HOLY TIME

HOLY TIME

MODERATE PURITANISM
AND THE SABBATH

JOHN H. PRIMUS

MERCER

ISBN 0-86554-340-2 [casebound]
ISBN 0-86554-350-X [paperback]

HOLY TIME
MODERATE PURITANISM AND THE SABBATH
Copyright © 1989
Mercer University Press
Macon, Georgia 31207
All rights reserved
Printed in the United States of America

The paper used in this publication meets
the minimum requirements of American National Standard
for Information Sciences—Permanence of Paper
for Printed Library Materials, ANSI Z39.48-1984.

LIBRARY OF CONGRESS CATALOGING-IN-PUBLICATION DATA

Primus, John H.
     Holy time : moderate Puritanism and the Sabbath / John H. Primus.
     viii + 184 pages   15 x 23 cm.   6 x 9″
     Includes bibliographies.
     ISBN 0-86554-340-2 (alk. paper).—ISBN 0-86554-350-X (pbk. : alk.
paper)
     1. Sabbath—History of doctrines—16th century. 2. Sabbath—
History of doctrines—17th century. 3. Puritans—England—History—16th century. 4. Puritans—England—History—17th century. I. title.
BV111.P75   1989   89-12471
263′.4′094109031—dc20   CIP

CONTENTS

PREFACE

This slender volume is not what I first had in mind. The world will simply have to wait for a comprehensive, definitive study of the origins of the Puritan Sabbath. Perhaps, in fact, there can be no such thing. In any case, my aims have become considerably more modest. A rather lively scholarly discussion about the Puritan Sabbath began in the 1970s and continues into the 1980s. I only wish to join in the conversation and to contribute another point of view to the discussion. And I hope that this re-examination of the relationship between the emerging Puritan movement and the phenomenon of Sabbatarianism will shed some additional light on the complex dynamics of the sixteenth-century Church of England.

The book is written not only for the specialists in Tudor Puritanism. I came to realize, when presenting a series of seminar papers on the topic to the colleagues in my department, none of them church historians, that there is a need for explaining this episode in Puritanism in such a way that it makes sense to persons in other theological disciplines. So I have attempted to write the essays, especially in part 2, in such a way that they may be intelligible to those uninitiated in the area. For this reason I have included contextual, explanatory paragraphs that briefly summarize and review events that are already well known to the experts.

Although the footnotes acknowledge my dependence upon those experts, I wish to mention a few of them whose work has been especially helpful to me: Patrick Collinson, Richard Greaves, Peter Lake, Kenneth Parker, Keith Sprunger, and Nicholas Tyacke. Their published works have been indispensable to this study, and from several of these people, personal notes and letters of encouragement and guidance have been most helpful.

I thank the administration and board of trustees of Calvin College for the two sabbatical leaves that enabled me to spend more than a year in England where most of the research was done. Life in Cambridge was an unmitigated joy for my wife and me, not only because of the place, but because of the people. There are many there who contributed to making my work pleasant and fruitful. I was consistently impressed with the friendly and efficient service provided by the staff of the Cambridge University Library, especially in the Rare Book Room and the Manuscripts Room. I appreciated the friendship and advice of Peter Brooks and Harry Porter, and of the faculty and staff at Westminster College. My wife and I found our British experience enriched by the friendship and warm hospitality of the Gardiners, the Longs, the Mailes, and the Wilsons, as well as by the pastor and several families at Eden chapel.

I express my appreciation also to my colleagues in the religion and theology department at Calvin College who have shown interest in this project and responded helpfully to portions of it. The Calvin Library staff always stood ready to help, and I owe a special word of thanks to Laetitia Yeandle of the Folger Library for help she graciously provided in deciphering a difficult manuscript. Finally, honorable mention must be made of two people who invested many, many hours in this undertaking from the very first draft to the last of many revisions. Donna Quist and Esther Vander Tuig, with unfailing cheer and skill, "processed the words" of the manuscript.

INTRODUCTION

NO REST FOR THE SABBATH

When the inimitable Thomas Fuller reflected on the flood of published material about the Sabbath day in England at the turn of the sixteenth and seventeenth centuries, he ruefully commented that "the sabbath itself had no rest."[1] Although that statement hardly seems applicable to the Christian church today when there is so little passionate discussion about either Sabbath theology or Sabbath observance, it is nonetheless a fact that on the academic level there has been a flurry of new interest in the phenomenon of English Sabbatarianism. In the mid-1960s Patrick Collinson wrote a short but useful article on the origins of Sabbatarianism. In 1970 Herbert Richardson made what must have seemed to many an outrageous suggestion—that the Puritan Sabbath should become the focal point of a new American theology; and since 1977 several additional articles have appeared as well as three books on English (and New England) Sabbatarianism, all by American authors.[2] These studies have been carefully and competently done, yet

---

[1]*The Church History of Britain* vol. 3 (London: Tegg and Son, 1837) 162.

[2]Patrick Collinson, "The Beginnings of English Sabbatarianism," vol. 1 of *Studies in Church History* (London: Nelson, 1964) 207-21; Herbert Richardson, *Toward an American Theology* (New York: Harper & Row, 1967); Winton Solberg, *Redeem the Time* (Cambridge: Harvard University Press, 1977); Richard Greaves, "The Origins of English Sabbatarian Thought," *Sixteenth Century Journal*, 12:3 (1981): 19-34; James T. Dennison, Jr., *The Market Day of the Soul* (Lanham MD: University Press of America, 1983); Kenneth L. Parker, *The English Sabbath: A Study of Doctrine and Discipline from the Reformation to the Civil War* (Cambridge University Press, 1988).

there are still some unsettled questions about the origin, meaning, and significance of the so-called Puritan Sabbath. Indeed, the more that is written, the more unsettled some of the questions have become.

Take, for example, the phrase "Puritan Sabbath." Once taken for granted, the phrase itself has become problematic and can be used to show where the current questions about the origins of English Sabbatarianism tend to focus. Since at least the middle of the seventeenth century, a close connection between Sabbatarianism and the Puritan movement in England was regarded as a historical given. In fact, it was once assumed that that relationship was so tight that the terms could almost be used interchangeably, or certainly in tandem, as in "the Puritan Sabbath."

This fundamental assumption has now been challenged. In his recent book, Kenneth L. Parker has argued that Sabbatarianism is by no means a Puritan invention.[3] "Puritanism" and "Sabbatarianism" are not words to be uttered in the same breath, for Sabbatarianism, as Parker defines it, antedates the Puritan movement. Parker argues that for three and a half centuries, we have blindly followed a historical model regarding the relationship of Puritanism and Sabbatarianism originally created by the seventeenth-century English royalist historian, Peter Heylyn. For self-serving purposes, or at least for crown-serving purposes, Heylyn, in his 1636 *History of the Sabbath*, developed an elaborate argument for an intimate connection between Puritanism and Sabbatarianism. Sabbatarianism, he declared, is a heresy concocted by those troublemaking, kingdom-threatening Puritans. Heylyn viewed Sabbatarianism as a late-sixteenth-century novelty, an innovation, a heterodox intrusion into orthodox English Protestant faith and life.

According to Parker, in Heylyn's fertile but suspicious mind there was yet another dimension to the Puritan-Sabbatarian connection. The Puritans, of course, had presbyterian leanings. In the 1570s, unable to achieve their aim to reform the Church of England radically within the confines of its Erastian authority structure, the Puritans mounted an attack on that hierarchical polity of the church. This presbyterian challenge constituted a serious threat to established ecclesiastical and political leadership, so the queen and her loyal and able archbishop, John Whitgift, effectively squelched the movement. But what is suppressed

[3]Parker, *English Sabbath*, 1-7.

in one place will bubble up again in another. Suppressed Presbyterianism was reincarnated in Sabbatarianism in the 1580s and 1590s. This Puritan-Presbyterian-Sabbatarian conspiracy was first suspected by Thomas Rogers, the anti-Presbyterian royalist chaplain of Archbishop Bancroft, Whitgift's successor. Rogers charged that Sabbatarianism was nothing more or less than Presbyterianism in clever disguise. A few decades later, Peter Heylyn picked up where Rogers left off, constructing a more elaborate and thorough argument designed to discredit the Puritans by charging them with the heresy of Sabbatarianism. In this perspective, Sabbatarianism was interpreted as the novel innovation of a radical sect of Puritans in the Church of England. Parker argues that both Rogers and Heylyn were guilty of highly biased, propagandistic accounts that have misled historians from the seventeenth century to the present.

Parker states the case more emphatically than others and heaps considerable blame on the rascals, Thomas Rogers and Peter Heylyn. But he is not the first to suggest caution about a one-to-one relationship between Puritanism and Sabbatarianism. As early as the 1920s, William Whitaker wrote an excellent work on the English Sabbath that begins with open skepticism about the assumption that Sabbatarianism originated with the Puritans.[4] And in most of the recent studies cited above, there is explicit acknowledgment of a lengthy process of development with regard to Sabbatarianism. Patrick Collinson advises that possible continental sources for Sabbatarianism should not be overlooked and, with specific regard to Rogers and Heylyn, states: "But Rogers's ingenious insinuation that Sabbatarianism was a new and cunning attempt at subversion of the established order by the Presbyterians was exploited by Peter Heylyn and repeated by Fuller and Jeremy Collier in their church histories, and so established itself as a plausible if not a sufficient account of the origins of English Sabbatarianism."[5] To call Parker's interpretation revisionist, therefore, may be overstating the case. And yet his work has reopened the fundamental question of the origin of Sabbatarianism and with it the even more critical issue of its relationship to Puritanism. Where did English Sabba-

---

[4]William B. Whitaker, *Sunday in Tudor and Stuart Time* (London: Houghton, 1933).

[5]Collinson, "Beginnings of Sabbatarianism," 221.

tarianism come from? Did it have continental connections? Was it a
departure from established Reformation theology? Where did it fit in
the larger English Reformation scene? What was the theological setting in which it developed? What was its purpose and function in the
church and commonwealth? What precisely was its relationship to Puritanism? This volume will explore these issues.

Parker has raised the problem of definition. What is Sabbatarianism? He uses the term very broadly and loosely to apply to almost any
situation in which concern is shown about the observance of a weekly
day of worship.[6] He is so insistent upon a continuity of Sabbath views
that reaches back into the Middle Ages, so emphatic about an English
Protestant consensus on the Sabbath, and so averse to the suggestion
of any theological and practical innovations at the end of the sixteenth
century that one is left wondering who these so-called Sabbatarians
were and whether they really existed. If Sabbatarianism was simply a
subjective projection arising out of the evil machinations of the likes of
Rogers and Heylyn, was there anything in the objective reality of late-
sixteenth-century England that corresponds to it at all?

Remarkably similar questions have been raised about Puritanism.
Since one of the purposes of this volume is to bring some new light to
bear on both Sabbatarianism and Puritanism and their relationship to
each other, and since the terms will be used regularly throughout, some
introductory reflections on the definitions of these problematic words
are appropriate.

There has been no end of discussion about the definition of Puritanism. Someone has observed that defining Puritanism is danger-
ously close to becoming an academic enterprise with a life of its own.[7]
The same cannot be said for Sabbatarianism. Little energy has been ex-
pended on that term. Recent studies have devoted minimal space to
definitions. And yet there are many formal similarities between the
terms *Puritan* and *Sabbatarian*. Both are tendentious labels, terms of
abuse, coined by hostile parties in an effort to prejudice opinion against
those so labeled. They are terms that arose in the nonscientific hubbub
of real life rather than out of studied reflection on life. They are street

[6]Parker, *English Sabbath,* 17ff., 41ff.

[7]Patrick Collinson, *English Puritanism* (London: The Historical Association, 1983) 6.

language rather than the language of the lecture hall. The words were coined in the heat of controversy rather than in a cool, detached academic setting.

It is important also to recognize that in the sixteenth century these labels were used for people, not for movements. Certain persons were designated Puritans or Sabbatarians; the more abstract terms *Puritanism* and *Sabbatarianism* arose later. Consequently, the most fitting historical approach to these terms is to discover who the people were who came to be called Puritans and Sabbatarians. We should define Puritanism and Sabbatarianism in terms of the Puritans and Sabbatarians, not vice versa.

There is a marvelous consensus on the answer to the question, "To whom was the term *Puritan* initially applied?" The word was first used in the 1560s as a label for English Protestant churchmen who were dissatisfied with the tempo and extent of reform in the church. The English Reformation was formally and externally a political act, the Act of Supremacy in 1534 by which Parliament removed the church in England from the jurisdiction of Rome and declared Henry VIII to be its supreme head. It was relatively easy, even natural, for the church to remain Roman Catholic in everything but name only. Some genuine reforms were initiated, however, for both political and religious-theological reasons. And yet a number of medieval practices, especially in the visible areas of the church's worship, were retained.

Two points of view soon surfaced. One was characterized by relative contentment with things as they were in the life of the church, and the other was characterized by a desire to seize the opportunity created by the separation from Rome in order to bring about genuine, complete reform. This more radical point of view was developed largely by people who had had some firsthand experience with reformation centers on the Continent, an experience which convinced them that they knew genuine reform when they saw it. They did not see it in England, so they called for the English church to return to the purity of the early New Testament church, which they believed was reflected in the purity of the best Reformed churches on the Continent. It was this passion for the purity of the church that led to their nickname. Puritans were defined as those "restlessly critical and occasionally rebellious members of the Church of England" who wanted a more purely

Reformed church, especially in the highly visible area of worship, and
secondarily in the area of church government as well.[8]

But what about Puritan*ism?* What faith lay behind the action? What
ideas and convictions account for the more radical approach to reform
of the church? What incited the Puritans to their opposition against
certain liturgical practices and against episcopal government? What
accounts for their powerful emphasis on "godly preaching" and,
eventually, on careful Sabbath observance? Richard Greaves takes a
step beyond the historical definition when he writes: "Puritans are ultimately and necessarily distinguishable from Anglicans not principally by their doctrine . . . but by the nature of their religious
experience, the thrust of which was the quest for an inner purity of heart
and mind, manifesting itself in spiritual warmth, aniconic worship, and
a frank acknowledgement of personal sinfulness and dependence on
the divine imputation of grace. . . . Puritanism was particularly a Spirit-
orientated faith that brought its adherents the conviction of internal
spiritual purity."[9]

Greaves argues that it was the nature and manifestation of this religious experience that made people Puritans. It involved a total spiritual reorientation expressed in hearing sermons, singing Psalms,

---

[8]Basil Hall, "Puritanism: The Problem of Definition," *Studies in Church History*, ed. Geoffrey J. Cuming (London: Thomas Nelson, 1965) 2:290. Others who
have given special attention to the problem of definition include: P. Collinson,
English Puritanism; idem, "A Comment: Concerning the Name Puritan," *Journal of Ecclesiastical History* 31 (October 1980): 483-88; Paul Christianson, "Reformers and the Church of England under Elizabeth I and the Early Stuarts,"
Journal of Ecclesiastical History 31 (October 1980): 463-82; William Hunt, *The Pu-
ritan Moment* (Cambridge: Harvard University Press, 1983); Richard Greaves,
Society and Religion in Elizabethan England (Minneapolis: University of Minne-
sota Press, 1981); Charles H. and Katherine George, *The Protestant Mind of the
English Reformation* (Princeton: Princeton University Press, 1981); Patrick
McGrath, *Papists and Puritan* (London: Blandford Press, 1967); James S. McGee,
The Godly Man in Stuart England (New Haven: Yale University Press, 1976);
Nicholas Tyacke, "Puritanism, Arminianism and Counter-Revolution," *The
Origins of the English Civil War*, ed. Conrad Russell (New York: Harper & Row,
1973); and Christopher Hill, *Society and Puritanism in Pre-Revolutionary England*
(New York: Schocken, 1964).

[9]Greaves, *Society and Religion*, 29.

reading Scripture, and joining in godly conversation. "This experience is the foundation on which all other characteristics of Puritanism rest."[10]

But again, what convictions lay behind not only the action but also the experience that Greaves describes as the heart of Puritanism? It is hard to improve upon an answer given more than three centuries ago by John Geree in 1646. "The old English Puritan," he said, "was such an one, that honored God above all, and under God gave every one his due."[11] This suggests that the touchstone of Puritanism was its authority model. That authority model was the Protestant principle applied with ferocious consistency. Only God is to be honored absolutely, and all authorities less than God are to be relativized. Since God reveals his authoritative will in the holy Scriptures, every practice, especially in the realm of the church and its worship, must be tested by the Bible. Ecclesiastical and civil authorities have their rightful place and must be honored, but always under God, whose will is revealed in the Bible.

So the Puritan with a Bible in his hand became a powerful, even potentially revolutionary force. The decisions and ordinances governing the church's life had to pass the biblical test. This did not mean, contrary to a stubborn misunderstanding about Puritanism, that only those things with express biblical warrant could be done in the church, but it did mean that even adiaphora had to meet biblical standards. To be acceptable practices for use in the church, they had to be inoffensive to all and orderly, comely, edifying to man, and glorifying to God.

It was this radically Protestant authority model—the will of God revealed in the Scriptures—that constituted what Collinson calls the "geological fault-line" between Puritans and Anglicans,[12] and that accounts for the Puritan position on liturgical matters, for the desire for a change in church government, and even for the central conviction, Sunday absolutism, that developed about the Sabbath. The model also accounts for the Puritans' overwhelming emphasis on the importance of preaching and their concern for purity of life, a life lived in accordance with the will of God in the Bible. Their single-minded aim was

[10]Ibid., 7.

[11]*The Character of an Old English Puritan* (London, 1646) 1.

[12]*English Puritanism*, 15–16.

to be godly people in a godly church in a godly nation, living the totality of their lives in the center of God's will, as expressed in the Scriptures. And if it be said that this description fails to distinguish Puritans
from the leading continental reformers, so be it. Puritans were simply
earnest and authentic Protestant reformers on English soil.

We turn now to the equally problematic term *Sabbatarian*. The first
and most obvious difficulty with this word lies in its ambiguity. According to any dictionary, a Sabbatarian is one who observes Saturday
as the day of rest and worship. Under this definition Jews and Seventh
Day Adventists, for example, are Sabbatarians. When the term was
applied to certain late-sixteenth- and seventeenth-century English reformers, however, it did not mean that at all—usually. For to compli-
cate the matter even more, in the heat of the early-seventeenth-century
Sabbath debates, a small radical fringe of Saturday Sabbatarians did
arise within the Church of England. These people, including John
Traske and Theophilus Brabourne, carried fourth commandment literalism to the extreme by calling upon the church to reverse a centu-
ries-old practice, and once again to observe Saturday as the God-
ordained day of rest and worship.

This reference to the radical Saturday Sabbatarians is not irrelevant. It should alert us to a significant fact: the term *Sabbatarian*, applied to people through the centuries, has always had at its heart the
issue of the appropriate *day* for worship. Even when the term came to
be applied to certain English Protestants who, like all other English
Protestants, worshiped on Sunday, it was nevertheless still an argument over the day of worship that constituted the definitive element
in the dispute.

This seems perfectly clear when we examine how the term was initially applied in late-sixteenth-century England. Its earliest documented appearance is in a sermon preached on 10 December 1599 by
Thomas Rogers at Bury St. Edmunds, just a stone's throw away from
arch-Sabbatarian Nicholas Bound's parish church at Norton in Sussex.
Notes taken by an anonymous auditor on that sermon have been preserved. The notes are sketchy and the handwriting difficult to deci-
pher, but the central thrust is clear. Rogers's main objection to the new
doctrines centered on what he took to be the absolutizing of a certain
day. The auditor heard him say,

That we Christians of the Church of England are bound to keep the Sabbath day is antichristian and unsound; 2. that the Sabbath is of the nature of tithes, of new moons, and Jewish feasts; 3. not possible to be proved that the Jews before the coming out of Egypt kept a Sabbath; 4. no certain day commanded for Christians in the Word of God more than other; 5. the Lord's day is not enjoined by God's commandment but by an human civil and ecclesiastical constitution. 6. He thinketh that the days commonly called the Lord's Days, Sabbath days or Sundays may be called the Queen's days and that he would so call them, and so did oftentimes in his sermon. 7. Those which hold that opinion against which he himself preached he called Sabbatarians and dominicans.[13]

Clearly, Rogers's main quarrel is with what we may call Sunday absolutism. This is especially apparent in points 4, 5, and 6. The Word of God designates no special day as our Christian Sabbath. Rather, what we call the "Lord's day" is established by the authority of church and state. Hence Sunday is more appropriately called the queen's day than the Lord's day.

A few years later, in his treatise on the doctrine and religion of the Church of England, Rogers speaks derisively of "our home Sabbatarians," people who have "set up a new idol, their Saint Sabbath . . . in the midst and minds of God's people."[14] Rogers also fashions a definition of sorts. Although stated in a highly prejudicial way, in it he clearly alludes again to the dispute about the day of worship, as well as to the developing tendency among the Sabbatarians toward legalistic observance of the day. He writes: "Their doctrine summarily may be reduced unto these two heads, whereof the one is that the Lord's day (even as the old Sabbath was of the Jews) must necessarily be kept and solemnized of all and every Christian under the pain of eternal condemnation both of body and soul. The other, that under the same penalty it must be kept from the highest to the lowest, both of king, and people, in sort and manner as these brethren among themselves have devised, decreed, and prescribed."[15]

---

[13]Townshend Papers, vol. 1, MS. 38492, fol. 104, The British Library.

[14]Thomas Rogers, *The Faith, Doctrine and Religion, Professed, and Protected in the Realme of England, and Dominions of the Same: Expressed in 39 Articles* (Cambridge, 1607) preface, par. 21. This work was later published by the Parker Society under the title, *The Catholic Doctrine of the Church of England* (Cambridge, 1854). Subsequent references will be to the Parker Society edition.

[15]Rogers, *Catholic Doctrine*, 19.

It may be true that Rogers had ulterior political motives for starting this fight, and it will be argued in a later chapter that his anti-Sabbatarianism may actually be as innovative as the Sabbatarianism that he is attacking. Yet when his definition is measured against Nicholas Bound's treatises on the Sabbath, it appears that Rogers is presenting at least an approximation of the truth. No matter how much continuity one sees in Sabbath teachings from the Middle Ages to the sixteenth century, one must concede on the basis of the sheer number of publications on the Sabbath after 1580 that there was a flurry of intense interest and concern about the Sabbath and an emphasis on the importance of Sabbath keeping that was, at least in degree of intensity, "new." This new intensity is accurately reflected in Rogers's definition when he refers to the extreme penalty for breaking the Sabbath. Furthermore, there was an inexorable drift toward more detailed prescriptions about how the Sabbath ought to be observed in the increasing and lengthening treatises on the Sabbath late in the century. This too is reflected in Rogers's description.

And finally, there is clear evidence that with respect to the doctrine of the Sabbath, the divine institution of Sunday as the New Testament Sabbath, while not entirely innovative, did stir up considerable new controversy beginning in the 1580s. This became a highly charged issue, indeed the most important one, because it brought the Sabbatarians into direct conflict with certain establishment figures who suspected that the Sabbatarians were using this doctrine to challenge the authority of church and state.

Current definitions of English Sabbatarianism tend to emphasize the belief in the moral, perpetual nature of the fourth commandment: "Remember the Sabbath day to keep it holy." Although in his book Parker does not carefully define the term, his entire argument hangs on the assumption that Sabbatarianism is essentially a commitment to the morally binding nature of the fourth commandment.[16] He tends to dismiss Sabbatarianism's most definitive element: its insistence on

---

[16]Parker's book is the published version of his Cambridge Ph.D. thesis where Sabbatarianism is defined in the dissertation abstract as "a commitment to the morally binding nature of the fourth commandment, ordained in God's creation by God's seventh day rest, and used in Christian tradition as a memorial of Christ's resurrection."

Sunday as the Christian Sabbath. Indeed, he regards this element as one of the "peripheral issues" surrounding the Sabbath.[17] It is precisely his broader and looser view of Sabbatarianism that enables Parker to construct an argument for a long "Sabbatarian" tradition in England and to disconnect it from Puritanism.

Collinson's definition also focuses on the moral-ceremonial question regarding the fourth commandment, but then moves on to include a reference to the Sunday Sabbath. He writes, "Sabbatarianism . . . is defined as something more than a certain ethical and social attitude to the use of Sunday: it implies the doctrinal assertion that the fourth commandment is not an obsolete ceremonial law of the Jews but a perpetual, moral law, binding on Christians; in other words, that the Christian observance of Sunday has its basis not in ecclesiastical tradition but in the decalogue."[18]

Greaves's definition is the most balanced and comprehensive. He first identifies Sabbatarianism as a "conviction that the fourth commandment is a perpetual, moral law originating with the creation and antedating the Mosaic law." He goes on to say, "Recognition of Sunday as the Christian Sabbath was reputed to be of divine and apostolic appointment, not ecclesiastical tradition." Finally, he adds, "Sabbatarianism also entailed the conviction that the entire day had to be set aside for the public and private exercise of religion, with no time devoted to labor, idleness, or recreation."[19] So in Greaves's definition, Sabbatarianism has three components: the moral nature of the fourth commandment, Sunday absolutism, and strict Sabbath observance. As Sabbatarian doctrine evolved in sixteenth-century England, all three of these elements eventually surfaced, most clearly in the works of Nicholas Bound, which must be regarded as the epitome of Sabbatarian doctrine.

In closing these reflections on definitions, let us return to the earlier observation that the terms *Puritan* and *Sabbatarian* were originally coined in the heat of battle. They were used to bludgeon opponents, not to analyze them. Therefore, we must be careful in our attempts to

---

[17]Parker, *English Sabbath*, 49.

[18]Collinson, "The Beginnings of English Sabbatarianism," 207.

[19]Greaves, "The Origins of English Sabbatarian Thought," 19.

attach precise, scientific definitions to the terms. To do so is to bring some distortion into our understanding of the complicated events of late-sixteenth-century England. The labels are terms of art rather than of science.[20] Consequently, for the cool, detached scholar writing an academic analysis of what transpired in the sixteenth century, the terms will always be somewhat elusive, imprecise, annoying, frustrating— and totally unavoidable.

The following chapters are divided into two parts. Part one is a brief historical sketch that, rather than attempting to duplicate Parker's extensive research, seeks to highlight certain developments and Sabbatarian emphases he tends to dismiss. It begins with a stage-setting chapter describing the high Sabbath views in England that are already evident in the early Reformation decades. This is followed by an account of the important Dedham debate in the 1580s, a pivotal episode signaling new developments in the understanding of the Sabbath. Then there is a discussion of the full-blown Sabbatarianism of a "Cambridge circle" of theologians late in the century. The historical section concludes in chapter 4 with a description of the anti-Sabbatarian reaction.

Part two consists of four independent, topical essays about various facets of English Sabbatarianism. The first of these (chap. 5) explores the broader theological environment in which Sabbatarianism arose and, using William Perkins as the model, analyzes how Sabbatarianism functioned within its theological context. The second essay (chap. 6) examines the Sabbath views of several continental reformers and discusses the legitimacy of Sabbatarian claims upon the reformers' support. Chapter 7 presents an analysis of Sabbatarian theology itself, isolating as the key to that theology the doctrine of the Trinity reflected in the Sabbatarian emphasis on creation, resurrection, and sanctification. The final chapter is a summary focusing on the central role of the Sabbath in the Puritan vision for a more fully reformed church in England.

My thesis is that while high Sabbath views were widespread in English Protestantism from the earliest years of the Reformation and were shared by conservative conformists and more radical Puritans alike, this

---

[20]Collinson, *English Puritanism,* 10.

consensus broke down in the 1580s and 1590s when there was a marked increase in the publication of Sabbath treatises, a more radical insistence on strict Sabbath observance, and a narrowing of the deuteronomic principle to the view that all the failures of the realm were attributable to Sabbath breaking. All of this led to the emergence of a genuine Sabbatarianism that reached its doctrinal apotheosis in Sunday absolutism—the view that the Old Testament Sabbath is continued in the New Testament first day of the week. It was especially this view that triggered the anti-Sabbatarian reaction which, in turn, contributed to the sharpening of division in the English church in the generation prior to the civil war and to the emergence of Anglicanism and Puritanism as distinct parties within the Church of England.

Parker is right, in other words, in his view of an early Sabbath consensus in England and even partly right in his thesis that Sabbatarianism was not a Puritan innovation; however, he is wrong in his argument that "Puritan Sabbatarianism" was therefore essentially the fraudulent invention of later Anglican propaganda. Sabbatarianism was much more than that. It was a well-developed position in its own right, and by the turn of the century was properly understood as intimately related to the Puritan movement. Failure to see this relationship is to be robbed of an important lens through which to view Puritanism and results in an impoverishment of our understanding of that movement.

This study is based primarily on an examination of printed sources from the sixteenth and seventeenth centuries. All quotations from these sources, except titles of books and treatises, have been modernized in spelling, punctuation, and capitalization.

I

1

THE
ENGLISH PROTESTANT
SABBATH TRADITION

PURITANISM AND SABBATARIANISM are intimately related. Puritan piety and Sabbatarian piety are nearly one and the same. By the end of the sixteenth century, Sabbatarianism had become the lynchpin in the Puritan program for more complete reform in England. But it is a mistake to believe that Sabbatarianism was simply and solely the direct offspring of the Puritan-Presbyterian movement in late-sixteenth-century England. There was not a cause-and-effect relationship between Puritanism and Sabbatarianism. Although he overstates his case, Kenneth Parker's work should effectively lay to rest this misguided view once and for all.

Sabbatarian tendencies are discernible in several early English reformers. Sunday absolutism is even apparent in the reformer who has been called a forerunner of Puritanism, John Hooper. There is considerable evidence that high Sabbath views were broadly accepted as protestant orthodoxy in the Church of England early in Elizabeth's reign, if not even earlier in the brief reign of Edward VI. The mature Sabbatarian views that developed after 1580 in greater detail and with increasing sophistication had their roots in these earlier decades of the English Reformation.[1]

---

[1]Kenneth Parker shows, in fact, that sixteenth-century English Sabbath doctrine and practice are basically consistent with medieval views of the Sabbath. *The English Sabbath*, 8-23.

JOHN HOOPER

John Hooper, who lived in exile in Zurich during the late years of
Henry VIII's reign, was ordained bishop of Gloucester and Worcester under Edward, and was martyred in the early years of the Marian interlude,
has been called the author of English Sabbatarianism.[2] His *Declaration of
the Ten Holy Commandments*, first published in 1548, was widely known
and used.[3] It went through two subsequent editions, the final one in 1588
during the period of immense interest in the Decalogue in general and
the Sabbath in particular. Hooper's interpretation of the fourth commandment represents the earliest articulation of explicit Sabbatarian views
in Protestant England.

The fourth commandment has several purposes, says Hooper. The
first is a spiritual purpose: "A Christian should upon this day call his in-
tendment and thoughts from the lusts, pleasures, vanities, and concu-
piscence of the world, unto the meditations of God and his works, to the
study of scripture, hearing of the word of God; to call upon God with ar-
dent prayer, to use and exercise the sacraments of God, to confer and give,
according to his ability, alms to the comforting of the poor."[4] All of the
elements included in later writings about Sabbath observance are mentioned here by Hooper, including meditation, Scripture reading, hearing
the Word, prayer, participation in the sacraments, and giving alms.

There is a second purpose for the fourth commandment—to offer time
for physical rest. Hooper emphasizes, somewhat more than the late-
century Sabbatarians, the need of both man and beast for regular in-
tervals of rest and repose. Otherwise, he writes, "They might never
endure the travail of the earth." God gave the Sabbath "not only that

---

[2]August Lang, *Puritanismus und Pietismus* (Darmstadt: Wissenschaftliche
Buchgesellschaft, 1972) 49. Regarding Hooper in general, see W. M. S. West,
"John Hooper and the Origins of Puritanism," *The Baptist Quarterly* 15 (1953-
1954) and 16 (1955-1956). West, however, in this series on Hooper as a forerunner of Puritanism does not deal with his Sabbatarianism.

[3]*Early Writings of John Hooper* (Cambridge: Parker Society, 1843) 255-430.

[4]Ibid., 337.

the body should be restored unto strength, and made able to sustain the travails of the week to come; but also that the soul and spirit of man, whiles the body is at rest, might upon the sabbath learn and know . . . the blessed will of his Maker."[5]

Then comes the theology. He states, "Almighty God therefore, not only in his commandments, but also at the first creation of the world, sanctified the seventh day, Gen ii.: that is to say, appointed it to an holy use, or separated it from other days, wherein men travail in the business of this world." This is not to say that Sunday is intrinsically more holy than any other day, and yet, he adds, "that day is always most holy in the which we most apply and give ourselves unto holy works." The division of life implied here between holy and profane is typical not only of Hooper but of the later Sabbatarians. It corresponds to the distinction made earlier between the "spiritual" and "physical" purposes of the fourth commandment. For Hooper, the Sabbath has a primary spiritual application, and yet there is, as well, an important social dimension to his Sabbath views in part because he links the fourth commandment to Creation. Hooper states, "The observation therefore of the sabbath doth extend as well unto the faith we have in God, as unto the charity of our neighbour; and not only that, but also unto the beasts that travail in our business and be our necessary servants, the which we should in no wise abuse, not only for their labour's sake, but also for the love of him that hath commended them unto our service, Almighty God."[6]

Hooper adds a third purpose for the Sabbath that is rarely emphasized by the later Sabbatarians. It is a "type and figure of the eternal and everlasting rest that is to come." He urges a careful reading of the fourth chapter of Hebrews. This passage provides the reason some do not enter into eternal rest: the "contempt of our captain's words, Jesus Christ" and failure to follow his commandments.[7]

Hooper stresses the need for householders to exercise firm social control over their servants and even the strangers "within thy port," seeing to it that they also properly observe the Sabbath and engage in rest and

---

[5]Ibid., 338.

[6]Ibid., 339.

[7]Ibid.

worship. He even gives the commandment an evangelistic turn when he argues that it is incumbent upon Christians to "teach a stranger the knowledge of God." He laments tendencies to give the stranger "the thing we owe him not, saving by the law of nature, and the thing that he may well lack, or else obtain of another, a supper or dinner for his money, or love; and never make mention of the thing we owe him, inasmuch as we be Christians. . . . Our office is to communicate the knowledge of God with him, so to move a communication, that the one might know the other's faith."[8]

The fourth commandment also has implications for civil authorities, according to Hooper. As the ancient Israelites were to compel the strangers within their borders to observe the Sabbath, so "every well-ordered commonwealth now in the time of the gospel should do the same, and constrain all people to hear the word of God, and see the ministration of their sacraments."[9]

Hooper employs the familiar scholastic distinction between "ceremonial" and "moral" in his analysis of the commandment. The "ceremony of the Sabbath" has been removed, says Hooper, but the rhythm of one day a week for worship is not abrogated. This moral element of the fourth commandment is "never to be abolished." The patriarchs, the prophets, and the Christians of the New Testament age have been given one day to rest from daily labor and to apply themselves to the "works of the Spirit; which secretly in ourselves should be done every day, with our handy labour." These works of the Spirit may be done openly on Sunday without the distraction of daily labor.[10]

Hooper includes a remarkable passage that anticipates one of the distinguishing elements of late-sixteenth-century Sabbatarianism: the divine appointment of Sunday as the new day of rest. He asserts, "This Sunday that we observe is not the commandment of man, as many say, that would, under the pretence of this one law, bind the church of Christ to all other laws— that men hath ungodly prescribed unto the church; but it is by express words commanded, that we should observe this day (the Sunday) for our sabbath, as the words of Saint Paul declareth, I Cor.

---

[8]Ibid., 340.

[9]Ibid., 341. The first use of the law is "civil" in Hooper's view. See 282.

[10]Ibid., 341, 342.

xvi, commanding every man to appoint his alms for the poor in the Sunday."[11] Hooper realizes the Corinthian passage needs some nimble interpreting to make it say what he wants it to say, so he quickly adds that when Paul says, "in one of the sabbath," this is "a Hebrew phrase, and is as much to say as, in the Sunday."[12] In Hooper's view, the day of worship was shifted to Sunday by divine appointment, a position lying at the heart of mature Sabbatarianism.

Hooper's adoption of the principle of Sunday absolutism can be understood and appreciated against the backdrop of the vestment controversy he initiated when, upon his appointment as bishop of Gloucester, he refused to don the surplice. At the heart of this dispute was the Reformation doctrine of *sola scriptura* and its application to the church.[13] Hooper took the position that nothing may be prescribed for the worship of the church that is not expressly commanded by the Scriptures. His opponents in the original vestment controversy used precisely such matters as *the time of worship* to illustrate their position that the church authorities do have a free hand in certain areas of decision-making in liturgical matters. It appears Hooper's insistence on "divine right" for every aspect of worship drove him to the most distinctive element of Sabbatarianism: the view that Sunday has been divinely, scripturally ordained as the Sabbath of the New Testament church.

It is remarkable to find this Sunday absolutism in Hooper. It gives additional credence to August Lang's labeling of Hooper as the author of English Sabbatarianism. Sabbatarian insistence on Sunday as the only proper day for worship is not simply an isolated piece of peculiar Puritan exegesis. It fits hand in glove with a fundamental concern about biblical authority for the rites of the church. Hooper's preoccupation with this theme is reflected in a later passage on the fourth commandment where he writes, "Sure we be that Christ, the patriarchs, prophets, and apostles, be saved, and believed no more, nor none otherwise, than they have left unto us by writings. Better it is to be certain of our doctrine and salvation with this holy church, than to associate ourselves with the rabble of liars, that boasteth and braggeth their abominable and ethnical cere-

---

[11]Ibid., 342.

[12]Ibid.

[13]John H. Primus, *The Vestments Controversy* (Kampen: J. H. Kok, 1960) 67.

monies, which be condemned in the scripture, to be laws for the holy church."[14] The Scriptures are the ultimate norm not only for the ruler but also for the people who lead the church. "God hath given thee the scripture to judge thy bishop, doctor, preacher, and curate, whether he preach gall or honey, his own laws or God's laws." Which, Hooper asks, was the "most pure church"—the church taught only by the simple text of the apostles, or the church taught for so many years by the "blind doctrine of men"? He answers, "They say, the holy church must be heard and obeyed. True it is: but our faith is not grounded upon those that be of the church, though they be the true ministers of God's word; but upon the word itself, as it appeareth, Matt. xvi."[15]

Clearly, these are seeds of revolutionary doctrine, sown in the context of Hooper's insistence upon divine right for the Sunday day of worship. Since this was written in Zurich in 1548, his attack was directed especially against "popery," but it is precisely the same argument he used later against the conservative hierarchy in the Church of England.

Hooper insists that the preaching of the Word is at the center of proper Sabbath observance, a theme that becomes so familiar in late-century writings on the Sabbath. He criticizes those who have abolished preaching in favor of the "massing and mumbling of canonical hours." But *God* understands us, these papists say. Perhaps, Hooper retorts, but God also understands "the cuckoo and the lowing of the cow," and they will hardly do for the worship of the church. Hooper adds that such "massing and mumbling" is a transgression of the fourth commandment, as is the preaching of false doctrine, improper administration of the sacraments, and the introduction of Jewish and "Aaronical" ceremonies into the church.[16]

For Hooper, neglecting social and ethical responsibilities on the Sabbath is also a serious abuse. This is where Hooper first raises the recreation issue. To be involved in "sports, games, and pastimes, keeping of markets and fairs upon the sabbath, is to abuse the sabbath." It is also a transgression of the fourth commandment to observe feasts for any saint. Hooper's essay concludes sharply with this sober warning: "The pain of

---

[14]*Early Writings of John Hooper*, 343.

[15]Ibid., 344.

[16]Ibid., 345, 346.

such as violate this commandment, and doth any vile work without necessity, is written Numb. xv., that he should be stoned to death." Without further comment or elaboration, the exposition abruptly ends.[17]

At least two definitive elements of later Sabbatarianism appear in Hooper's interpretation: emphasis on the creation origin of the Sabbath commandment, which gives it perpetual, moral significance, and the express divine appointment of Sunday as the New Testament Sabbath. Neither of these doctrines is treated at great length, but both points are made in addition to a rather punctilious recital of Sabbath obligations.

Later in the century these views would create dissent and dispute in the Church of England. In Hooper's tumultuous times, when the church had so recently been declared independent of Rome, there were far too many other matters of practical reform that needed immediate attention. Meanwhile, Hooper's strong Sabbath emphasis, at least on the practical side, was apparently compatible with the English Protestant mind that was developing by mid-century. There is additional evidence, as the following sections will demonstrate, that this mind incorporated a high view of the Sabbath.

LATIMER, PONET, BECON, AND NOWELL

Hugh Latimer, who was once, by his own testimony, "as obstinate a papist as any was in England," became one of the earliest of the Cambridge reformers. He later was bishop of Worcester and, like Hooper, was martyred under Mary in 1555. A powerful preacher, he comments in a sermon preached in Lincolnshire in 1553 on the proper observance of the Sabbath.[18] In the context of a paragraph exalting the importance of preaching, he declares that "the holy day is ordained and appointed to none other thing, but that we should at that day hear the word of God, and exercise ourselves in all godliness." It is not a day for "feasting, drinking, or gaming, or such foolishness," but is a "day appointed of God that we should hear his word, and learn his laws, and so serve him." Since "Sundays are appointed to preaching," God commands that "we shall

---

[17]Ibid., 348.

[18]*Sermons by Hugh Latimer* (Cambridge: Parker Society, 1844) 471-73.

abstain from working" and that we sanctify or hallow the day. It is a "marriage-day, wherein we are married unto God; which day is very needful to be kept." It is not a day for "belly-cheer," yet "there is no wickedness, no rebellion, no lechery, but she hath most commonly her beginning upon the holy-day."

To reinforce his strong view of Sabbath keeping, Latimer also refers to the severe punishment of the Sabbath stick gatherer in Numbers 15, "which thing is an ensample for us to take heed, that we transgress not the law of the sabbath-day." Contemporary Sabbath breakers will be similarly punished one day, "either here, or else in the other world, where the punishment shall be everlasting." Since God "is and remaineth still the old God: he will have us to keep his sabbath, as well now as then." Again with reference to the Numbers account, Latimer declares that through it God gives "a warning unto the whole world by that man, that all the world should keep holy his sabbath-day." Latimer's emphasis is almost exclusively on practical issues of Sabbath observance, but it is nonetheless clear that for him the fourth commandment continues to be relevant to the New Testament church.

The *Catechismus Brevis*, written near the end of Edward's reign and usually ascribed to John Ponet, makes this firm statement about the Sabbath: "Last of all this ought we to hold stedfastly and with devout conscience, that we keep holily and religiously the sabbath day; which was appointed out from the other for rest and service of God."[19] The view that the Sabbath rest in particular is ceremonial is not suggested. In addition, the catechism stresses, in Genevan fashion, the continued New Testament applicability and function of the law in the context of the covenant between God and his people.

Thomas Becon, Archbishop Cranmer's chaplain, was not an undiluted Sabbatarian but displayed tendencies in that direction. According to Becon, the whole law is still binding on the New Testament Christian community. This includes the fourth commandment, to which Becon devoted six pages in his widely used catechism published in 1560.[20] The fourth commandment "requesteth of us two things: First, that we keep holy the sabbath-day: Secondly, that on the seventh day we rest from all

---

[19]*Two Liturgies and Other Documents in the Reign of King Edward VI* (Cambridge: Parker Society, 1844) 497.

[20]*The Catechism of Thomas Becon* (Cambridge: Parker Society, 1844) 80-85.

worldly and bodily business, labours, and works, that we may the more freely serve the Lord our God, and consider the things which appertain unto the salvation of our souls." Becon's advice on how to sanctify the day contains a lengthy recital of prohibitions similar to those that appear with such frequency later in the century: lewd pastimes, banqueting, dicing, carding, dancing, bear-baiting, bowling, shooting, laughing and whoring, bargaining, buying and selling, and the keeping of fairs and markets. The mind and body must be free of such diversions so that they can be wholly dedicated to "godly and spiritual exercises." These exercises contain the familiar elements of meditation and reflection on God's greatness and goodness, hearing the Word, prayer, sacraments, and "visiting, counselling, comforting, and helping of the poor and miserably afflicted persons." Becon regarded the Jewish Sabbath as partly ceremonial, "as touching the external rest, and the self seventh day." At the same time, Becon does not hesitate to call Sunday "the sabbath of the Christians."

One of the most important and influential catechisms of the Elizabethan period was the one written by Alexander Nowell, dean of St. Paul's from 1560 until his death in 1602.[21] Nowell wrote it early in the 1560s, and it was authorized by Convocation in 1563, thereby receiving official status "for the bringing up of the youth in godliness, in the schools of the whole realm." Its publication, however, was delayed until 1570. Similar in many ways to both the Genevan Catechism and the *Catechismus Brevis*, it does have a more extended treatment of the fourth commandment than either of these catechisms.

The Sabbath "is appointed only for the worshipping of God"; hence "the godly must lay aside all worldly business, that they may the more diligently attend to religion and godliness." God himself is an example of Sabbath keeping, for he rested on the seventh day and "notable and noble examples do more thoroughly stir up and sharpen men's minds." Furthermore, "nothing is more to be desired of men than to frame themselves to the example and imitation of God." There is a ceremonial aspect to the commandment that "belonged peculiarly to the Jews," but we continue to be bound to the law according to its three perpetual uses: "first to stablish and maintain an ecclesiastical discipline, and a certain order of the Christian commonweal; secondly, to provide for the state of servants,

---

[21]*A Catechism by Alexander Nowell* (Cambridge: Parker Society, 1853).

that it be made tolerable; thirdly, to express a certain form and figure of the spiritual rest." By "ecclesiastical discipline," Nowell means the entire pattern of public worship, prayer, preaching, and the sacraments. It is "for our negligence and weakness' sake" that "one certain special day is, by public order, appointed for this matter."[22]

The stress on the servants' rest is stronger than in any of the other concurrent statements on the Sabbath. As Nowell observes, "They which be under other men's power should have some time to rest from labour. For else their state should be too grievous and too hard to bear." After all, it is in the best interests of the masters too to give servants a time to rest so "after respiting their work awhile, they may return more fresh and lusty to it again." Of course, a spiritual resting from sin is also required by the Sabbath law, but the catechism sets this in the context of the literal, physical Sabbath rest. It is when "resting from worldly business and from our own works and studies, and as it were having a certain holy vacation" that "we yield ourselves wholly to God's governance, that he may do his works in us." While the latter should be done on the other days of the week also, this does not obviate the need for a special day of rest and worship.[23]

These four brief examples serve to illustrate that many of the strong Sabbath views of John Hooper were shared by other English protestant leaders. At the same time, it is important to notice that the most distinctive element of Sabbatarianism is missing in these examples. Thomas Becon comes close when he refers to Sunday as the Christian's Sabbath, but none of the four explicitly asserts that the first day of the week is the Sabbath by divine appointment. It is not until the 1590s that this unique doctrine explicitly reappears.

HOMILY OF THE PLACE AND TIME OF PRAYER

In the early 1560s, soon after the reestablishment of Protestantism, two books of homilies were published under the aegis of Queen Elizabeth and her first archbishop, Matthew Parker. The first part contained homilies used during the reign of Edward VI; the second added still more homilies, many of which may have been written or were in early stages of

---

[22]Ibid., 128, 129.

[23]Ibid., 129.

preparation in the late years of Edward's reign. These homilies were designed for use in all of the churches, especially to supply a need created by "ministers who have not the gift of preaching." All ministers were required "to read and declare to their parishioners plainly and distinctly one of the said Homilies in such order as they stand in the book."[24] These homilies therefore represent many aspects of official religious thought in Elizabethan England.

Included in the second book is "An Homily of the Place and Time of Prayer," possibly written by John Jewel.[25] This homily provides much grist for the mill of later Sabbatarians, for it contains, though not without moments of ambiguity, some hints of Sabbatarian theology. It affirms that the fourth commandment contains ceremonial ingredients but also elements "appertaining to the law of nature"—hence moral, perpetually binding law that requires Christians to keep one day a week as a day of rest from physical labor. This "law of nature" is rooted in two things: God's "express charge" that "upon the Sabbath day, which is now our Sunday," we must cease from "all weekly and workday labour," and God's example in the creation of the world. The homily verges on declaring that a weekly day of physical rest is a creation ordinance. The shift from seventh day to first day also appears to be an ecclesiastical tradition with biblical roots. "Our Sunday" is explicitly referred to as "the Sabbath day." The practice of using the first day of the week is a response of "godly Christian people" to the "example and commandment of God." The homily appeals to apostolic practice for support, including a reference to the Book of Revelation where the apostle John speaks of "the Lord's Day."[26]

The homily continues with a cranky recital of Sabbath abuses worthy of a Philip Stubbes or a John Field.[27] "But, alas, . . . it is lamentable to see the wicked boldness of those . . . who pass nothing at all of keeping and hallowing the Sunday." There are those who shamelessly do their busi-

---

[24]*The Two Books of Homilies Appointed to Be Read in Churches* (Oxford: Oxford University Press, 1859) 3, 5.

[25]Jewel is commonly believed to be the editor of the whole as well as author of some of the homilies. Cf. editor's preface, xvii and xxxiii.

[26]Ibid., 339, 340.

[27]See below, 32-36.

ness on Sunday, who "ride and journey," "drive and carry," "row and ferry," "buy and sell," and "keep markets and fairs," using Sunday as any other day. There are others still worse for, although they do not labor on the Sabbath, "they rest in ungodliness and in filthiness, prancing in their pride, pranking and pricking, pointing and painting themselves, to be gorgeous and gay; they rest in excess and superfluity, in gluttony and drunkenness, like rats and swine; they rest in brawling and railing, in quarrelling and fighting; they rest in wantonness, in toyish taling, in filthy fleshliness; so that it doth too evidently appear that God is more dishonoured and the devil better served on the Sunday than upon all the days in the week beside."[28] The last part of this charge was taken up almost verbatim by later Sabbatarians. Following the example of Hooper and Latimer, the homily also refers to Numbers 15 and its solemn warning about God's capital punishment of Sabbath breakers.

Since this is a homily about place as well as time, it goes on to urge the people to public worship in the church in order to "sanctify the Sabbath day, that is the Sunday, the day of holy rest." Again, Sunday is identified as the Sabbath day. In the churches God's people are "to give themselves to holy rest and contemplation, pertaining to the service of Almighty God: whereby we may reconcile ourselves to God, be partakers of his reverent Sacraments, and be devout hearers of his holy word."[29] No more is said about the content of worship, undoubtedly because this is treated to some extent in succeeding homilies. But enough has been quoted to demonstrate that both the content and the strident tone of the homily are somewhat reminiscent of the later exponents of a strict Sabbath who came to be known as Sabbatarians. Although the Sabbatarian nuances are more subtle than those in the later, more fully developed Sabbatarian writings, the homily demonstrates that there was a thread of continuity between late-sixteenth-century Puritan Sabbatarianism and earlier, perfectly proper and official English Protestant views.

THE SABBATH JEREMIADS

We have already noticed the tendencies in some early interpretations of the Sabbath—most notably in the "Homily of the Place and Time of

---

[28]Ibid., 341.

[29]Ibid., 344, 345.

Prayer" and in Thomas Becon's catechism—to compile catalogs of Sabbath sins. This tendency became a full-blown practice in the 1570s and 1580s. A number of sermons and tracts preached and published during this time capitalize on the Sabbath-breaking theme. There is a measure of Sabbath theology in these sermons, but they are more concerned with Sabbath observance and represent a developing art form—the Sabbath jeremiad.

The high incidence of these jeremiads in the 1570s and early 1580s suggests that in those years the Sabbatarian temperature was rising in England. They also illustrate the rapidly developing practice of linking the deuteronomic principle to Sabbath breaking. God will punish the people of England if they do not keep his commandments, especially the fourth commandment!

One of the first jeremiads appeared in 1572, in the form of a lengthy sermon by Humphrey Roberts entitled *An Earnest Complaint of Divers Vain, Wicked and Abused Exercises Practised on the Saboth Day*.[30] It contains a minimum of Sabbatarian theology. The fourth commandment has a moral element that "doth still remain and ought of Christians to be obeyed, and kept." The Sabbath is a reminder of our "deliverance from the bondage of Satan and everlasting death and also of our everlasting rest." On the change of day, Roberts states that "our Sabbath is appointed upon that day in which Christ rose from death . . . which the Christians name *Dies Dominicus:* the Lord's day." This day is "to be wholly bestowed in the Lord's service."[31]

Most of the sermon is devoted to lengthy complaints about various forms of Sabbath neglect, which for Roberts is the chief cause of sin in the realm and of the failure of the English church to achieve full reformation. "For truly, the abusing of the Sabbath day, in this our time, is a great cause, that Satan so much prevaileth in his wicked practices: wherewith he would hinder the Gospel, and cause ignorance still to remain."[32] Neglect of the Sabbath means failure "to hear the gospel preached," accounting for the "ignorance" so prevalent in the land. Consequently, Sabbath breakers must be punished just as certainly as thieves and murderers. The "same

---

[30](London, 1572).

[31]Ibid., fol. C1.

[32]Ibid., fols. B1, B2.

God that said: Thou shalt not steal, said also: Remember thou keep holy the Sabbath day. So that in God's sight, it is as great an offense to violate the Sabbath day, as it is to steal, or such like."[33]

John Northbrooke wrote a tract published in 1577 entitled *A Treatise wherein Dicing, Dauncing, Vaine Playes or Enterluds with Other Idle Pastimes, &. Commonly Used on the Sabboth Day, Are Reproved by the Authorities of the Word of God and Auntient Writers.*[34] Northbrooke sets his lengthy and tedious dialogue between "Age" and "Youth" in the context of the deuteronomic covenant with God, with heavy emphasis on humanity's obligation to obey and keep the covenant. Especially fierce punishment is threatened for anyone who "negligently heareth the word of God."[35]

With appeals to Brentius and Bullinger, Northbrooke interprets the kind of idleness required on the Sabbath—an idleness from carnal pleasure, and an idleness that will make people more apt and able to work in their ordinary callings. But idleness is no end in itself. God's rest is the model, and he rested "from creating, but not from governing and ordering" the creation.[36] In classic Sabbatarian style Northbrooke declares that "the whole keeping of the law standeth in the true use of the sabbath."[37] He may have been the first to find special significance in the positioning of the fourth commandment between the first and second tables of the law. It is a commandment, he observes, involving both faith in God and love toward man, therefore both "the first and second table are therein contained."[38] He also argues that there are essentially three Sabbaths, or three uses of the Sabbath: corporal rest, spiritual resting from sin, and heavenly rest—"that is, after this our pilgrimage and end of our life, we shall keep our sabbath and rest in heaven with Jesus Christ for ever and ever."[39]

---

[33]Ibid., fol. D4.

[34](London, 1577). This sermon was edited by J. P. Collier for the Shakespeare Society, London, 1843.

[35]Ibid., 7, 10.

[36]Ibid., 39, 40.

[37]Ibid., 42.

[38]Ibid., 43.

[39]Ibid., 43, 44.

In August of 1578, Paul's Cross in London provided the platform for John Stockwood's lament about Sabbath breaking in an incredibly lengthy sermon on Acts 10:1-8, the story of Cornelius.[40] (He admits in the "Admonition to the Reader" that he was unable to preach it all at one sitting.) Regarding the Sabbath, Stockwood states his case in words reminiscent of the "Homily of the Time and Place of Prayer." "I dare boldly stand to avouch it," he says, "that there is no day in the week, wherein God is so much dishonored, as on that day when he should be best served."[41]

The doctrine of the covenant becomes the larger setting in which his material is handled. King Josiah in 2 Kings 23:2-3 is a worthy model for English monarchs. Josiah read the law to all his subjects "and caused all to make a covenant, that they would walk according to that which they understood the Lord to require at their hand."[42] But in England, Sabbath abuse was a leading sign of failure to walk in God's ways. The perverse desires of most citizens were such that on the Lord's day they "must have fairs kept, must have bear-baiting, bull baiting (as if it were a thing of necessity for the bears of Paris-garden to be baited on the Sunday) must have bawdy Enterludes, silver games, dicing, carding, tabling, dancing, drinking, and what I pray you is the penalty of the offender herein, forsooth a slap with a foretail."[43]

The sermon heavily emphasizes the responsibilities of those in leadership positions to use their influence to bring about obedience to the Sabbath commandment and to all other laws of the covenant in order to insure the blessing of God on the realm. Let the queen follow the example of King Josiah: that she may be willing to hear the law of God and "may be careful to cause all her subjects to make a covenant, to walk after the commandments of the Lord."[44] Heads of households are to provide religious instruction for all within their jurisdiction. Stockwood pleads with the lord mayor of London and other magistrates to bring honesty,

---

[40]*A Sermon Preached at Paules Crosse on Barthelmew Day, Being the 24. of August, 1578* (London, 1578).

[41]Ibid., 51.

[42]Ibid., 73.

[43]Ibid., 50. Cf. 86.

[44]Ibid., 79.

virtue, and godliness to the city. "Thus doing, the Lord will bless you with many blessings, both you and your City."[45]

Stockwood's concern about the Sabbath centers in the need to hear the Word. He excoriates those who fail to "resort to the place of preaching" on the Lord's Day, and even those who do attend services on Sabbath morning, but in the afternoon think "that without all controlment, they may run after all kinds of vanity." They must resist the devil who "inventeth many kind of vain exercises for that day, to pull them from hearing of the word." The "better parts" of the Lord's day are "horribly profaned by devilish inventions" like dancing and May poles, "insomuch that in some places, they shame not in the time of divine service, to come and dance about the church, and without to have men naked dancing in nets, which is most filthy."[46]

Stockwood regards the theater as another threat to the Sabbath. He questions "whether in a Christian commonwealth [plays] be tolerable on the Lord's Day."[47] Stewardship of time is one of the moral issues raised in connection with the legitimacy of plays. With reference to the theater, Stockwood complains of the "loss of time which Paul willeth us to redeem . . . and who is he that is so evil, as to affirm two hours spent in hearing a bawdy play, which should be spent in hearing a sermon, to be the redeeming of time?"[48]

Few treatises on the Sabbath can match the sheer gloominess of those written by John Field and Phillip Stubbes. Both were prepared and published at about the same time in 1583. John Field, "the Lenin of Elizabethan puritanism,"[49] recounts with restrained glee a Sabbath-day sporting disaster. The title of his tract sums up the story: *A Godly Exhortation by Occasion of the Late Judgement of God, Shewed at Parris-garden, the Thirteenth Day of Januarie: Where Were Assembled by Estimation; above a Thousand Persons, whereof Some Were Slaine, & of that Number, at the Least, as Is Crediblie Reported, the Thirde Person Maimed and Hurt.*[50]

[45]Ibid., 86, 87.

[46]Ibid., 132, 133, 134.

[47]Ibid., 135.

[48]Ibid., 137.

[49]Patrick Collinson, *Archbishop Grindal* (London: Jonathan Cape, 1979) 169.

[50](London: 1583). There is no pagination of any kind in this treatise, hence no further footnoting of the following quotations.

On 13 January 1583, in a stadium outside London, hundreds of people were assembled for an exciting afternoon of bear baiting. It was, of
course, the Sabbath, "in the time of common prayers." The grandstands
were packed and the ancient structure could not take the weight. "This
gallery that was double, and so compassed the yard round about, was so
shaken at the foundation, that it fell as it were in a moment flat to the
ground, without post or piece, that was left standing, so high as the stake
whereunto the Bear was tied." Field admits that the stadium was old and
rotten, and therefore a secondary natural cause was involved. But it was
nevertheless "an extraordinary judgment of God, both for the punishment of these present prophaners of the Lord's Day that were there, and
also to inform and warn us that were abroad." Five men and two women
were killed, all of whom he names. Several were servants, a convenient
reminder of that part of the commandment requiring masters to ensure
that servants also be engaged in worship on the Sabbath.

One of the most significant aspects of Field's treatise is the manner in
which he sets his judgments within the framework of the deuteronomic
covenant between God and the nation. He states that England has been
abundantly blessed both materially and spiritually: "This little land as a
garden of the Lord" has been "decked and garnished with sundry most
gracious and excellent gifts." God "hath set us as it were in the paradise
of the world," he continues, for there is abundance of grain, precious
metals, peace, protection and quietness. "Our princes sit in the gates, and
our nobility ride in chariots and coaches." Clearly, "God hath given himself unto us to be our God, and hath chosen us to be his people." He has
given his son Jesus Christ who sets us in a new covenant relationship with
God. "The Jews were his people by a conditional covenant . . . but we
are his people adopted, assured in a new covenant, sealed in the blood
and obedience of Jesus Christ, the end of all the promises." Indeed, "Our
benefits have been greater, than ever were bestowed upon any nation ex-
cepting neither one or other." But Field questions whether the people are
responding gratefully to and walking worthily of these benefits. Of course,
Field says, they are not. The whole world, in his eyes, is becoming increasingly secularized: "We are come to the dotage of the world, set on
mischief, and growing to worse and worse." Sabbath keeping is a prime
illustration of this growing secularization. He states, "Is it not a lamentable thing, that after so long preaching of the gospel, there should be so
great prophanation among us? That theatres should be full, and churches

be empty? That the streets should be replenished, and the places of holy exercises, left destitute? . . . For admit that the thing itself were a recreation, lawful by the word of God: yet who will grant it upon the Lord's Sabbath?" Even though "preachers have cried out, from time to time for the reformation of such prophanation, yet there hath been little or no amendment at all."

As in ancient Israel, so in England the people break the commandments and worship false idols. There is swearing, lying, superstition, but above all, Sabbath breaking in the land. The Sabbath is made for the "solemn assemblies of God's saints," but it is defiled even by churchgoers when they have profane thoughts and worship without adequate preparation. Field clearly is going to have his day even if he has to invade the area of "men's thoughts" to do so.

There are others who give to God only "some little piece" of the Sabbath, spending the balance of the day in personal pleasures and "wicked pastimes with all greediness." Instead of "gadding to sermons," there is "gadding to all kinds of gaming, and there is no tavern or alehouse, if the drink be strong, that lacketh any company: there is no dicing house, bowling alley, cock pit, or theatre, that can be found empty." Nothing keeps the people away from these bawdy places, whether fear of danger, loss of time, or expense. In church, "three pence, five pence, a shilling or two" required to maintain the preaching "is a great matter and wonderful burden, much humming and hawing about it: but pounds and hundreds can be well enough afforded, in following these least pleasures."

In one of his only theological comments about the fourth commandment, Field affirms the moral character of Exodus 20 in general. He admits that there is an element of the fourth commandment peculiar to the Jews, "but there is yet a day to be kept" for the sake of both soul and body. And when we break the Sabbath as it was broken at Paris-garden, "the wrath of God must needs be poured out against us."

So he calls not simply on individuals to repent, but on the whole nation which is in covenant with God. "O England, repent, thou that hast tasted of so many blessings, and yet hast provoked God with so many sins." In keeping with this national, civil view of the covenant, he dedicates the treatise to the mayor of London and to the "Sargeant at the Law" who is one of the queen's "justices of peace and quorum." The Paris-garden disaster and the sins that caused it "most concerneth you, and such as are in authority. For who are more specially bound to look unto the observation of the laws of God, than the magistrates, who are set up as conductors and leaders of the people, instead of God." This utterance reflects a commitment to proper civil order that often served to keep in check the revolutionary tendencies of the English Puritans.

The year 1583 also saw the publication of Phillip Stubbes's famous diatribe *The Anatomie of Abuses*.[51] He begins, like Field, with a reference to England's blessings. "The Lord hath blessed that land, with the knowledge of his truth above all other lands in the world, yet is there not a people more abrupt, wicked, or perverse, living upon the face of the earth."[52] After that promising opening, he goes on to catalog the abuses, one of which is abuse of the Sabbath day. While some sanctify the day with the proper exercises of public worship, others spend the day

> in frequenting of bawdy stage-plays and interludes, in maintaining Lords of misrule (for so they call a certain kind of play which they use), May games, Church-ales, feasts, and wakes; in piping, dancing, dicing, carding, bowling, tennis playing; in bear-baiting, cock-fighting, hawking, hunting, and such like; in keeping of fairs and markets on the Sabbath; in keeping courts and leets; in football playing, and such other devilish pastimes; reading of lascivious and wanton books, and an infinite number of such like practices and profane exercises used upon that day whereby the Lord God is dishonoured and his Sabbath violated.[53]

Theology is not Stubbes's strong suit, but he does briefly develop a position that touches on one of Sabbatarianism's central elements. God created in six days and rested on the seventh, "and therefore he commanded that the seventh day should be kept holy in all ages to the end of the world." At Sinai, two thousand years later, God iterated this commandment. There are four reasons or causes for the Sabbath law: to put us in mind of God's creative workmanship; that his Word "might be preached, interpreted, and expounded" to the assembled church; to grant repose from labor for both man and beast so that "they might the better sustain the travails of the week to ensue"; and to provide a type and fig-

---

[51](London, 1583).

[52]Ibid., fol. Biii.

[53]Ibid., fol. Lii.

ure of the blessed rest of eternity.[54] This passage, among others, is strongly reminiscent of John Hooper's *Declaration of the Ten Commandments*, which was republished just a few years later.

Stubbes writes with passion and color when he speaks of sin and abuses "sucked out of the Devil's teats." He excoriates dancing in these terms: "What clipping, what culling, what kissing and bussing, what smooching and slabbering one of another, what filthy groping and unclean handling is not practiced everywhere in these dancings." With vivid horror he describes the dire consequences of breaking the Sabbath: "So shall they be stoned, yea grinded to pieces for their contempt of the Lord in his Sabbath."[55]

It is not the nature of jeremiads to blaze new trails, but rather to bemoan departures from old ones. The rash of Sabbath jeremiads in the 1570s and 1580s, therefore, do not represent an attempt to set forth a new view of the Sabbath. They are, rather, lengthy laments about tragic departures from a strong Sabbath tradition, and passionate pleas to return to that tradition. The large number of these pleas appearing in the 1570s, however, does indicate a new intensity of concern about the Sabbath. The jeremiads gave the fourth commandment higher visibility, which is always an invitation to discussion and dispute. Although Christian Sabbath keeping was taken seriously from the earliest days of the Reformation in England, in the 1580s and 1590s the interpretation of the fourth commandment did become a topic of discussion and dispute. It was in this new context of controversy that Sabbatarian theology was more carefully and sharply developed.

----

[54]Ibid.

[55]Ibid.

2

THE
DEDHAM
SABBATH DEBATE*

SOME SEVENTY MILES northeast of London, near the Stour river in John Constable country, lies the village of Dedham. From the center of the village rises the stately tower of the Dedham church, which can be seen deep in the distance in a number of Constable's landscapes. It was here in 1582 that a group of clergy from Dedham and surrounding parishes in the Essex countryside organized into a "conference" of pastors.[1] The initial membership of thirteen "godly brethren" agreed to meet monthly to confer about the Scriptures and to deal with practical problems they were facing in their parishes. Approximately one hour was to be devoted to preaching and prayer. One of the members was assigned each month to preach on a scriptural passage, and discussion would follow. The remainder of the monthly conference was typically spent discussing matters of mutual concern pertaining to pastoral work

---

*This chapter is a revised version of an article originally published in *Sixteenth Century Journal* as "The Dedham Sabbath Debate: More Light on English Sabbatarianism."

[1]Roland G. Usher, *The Presbyterian Movement in the Reign of Queen Elizabeth* (London: Royal Historical Society, 1905); Patrick Collinson, *The Elizabethan Puritan Movement* (Berkeley and Los Angeles: University of California Press, 1967) 222-39.

in the parishes, although some of the meetings were dedicated wholly to prayer and fasting. The Dedham conference was organized 22 October 1582 and the Puritan pastors in this area met regularly thereafter for the next seven years.

The Dedham conference was one of several scattered about the country, organized by Church of England clergy sympathetic with the presbyterian movement. The conferences, whether deliberately or not, were mini-experiments in Presbyterianism, for they incorporated the ideas of local organization and decision making. While it should not be assumed that they were organized primarily to subvert episcopacy and establish Presbyterianism, it certainly *looked* that way to the authorities in Canterbury and London. As a result of pressure from these authorities, the Dedham conference came to an end in 1589 after seven years of regular meetings. The minutes conclude with a lament: "Thus long continued through God's mercy this blessed meeting and now it ended by the malice of Satan, some cause of it was complaints against us preferred to the Bishop of London."

Fortunately, the conferees did not shred their papers. Richard Parker, vicar of the Dedham church, was the secretary of the organization. He took notes of the proceedings and collected correspondence and other papers. Many years later, in 1604, Parker transcribed the notes into an orderly account to which he attached the letters and papers. This invaluable Dedham collection is now in the John Rylands Library in Manchester.[2] Much of the material has been deciphered, edited, and published by Roland Usher in a small volume entitled *The Presbyterian Movement.*

Some of the items, however, have not been published, among them two substantial papers on the Sabbath that provide an invaluable record of the sharp conflict of opinion within the Dedham conference relative to the understanding of the Sabbath.[3] These papers are of crucial importance in the history of the English Sabbath, for there is no earlier comparable record of serious dispute about the Sabbath in England. The Dedham debate is the earliest indication of a breakdown in the En-

---

[2]Rylands English MS 874. Collinson says that without the Dedham collection, we would hardly be able to write the history of the sixteenth-century classical-presbyterian movement in England.

[3]Ibid., fols. 237-47.

glish consensus regarding the Sabbath. As the debate develops, it suggests some connection between Sabbatarianism and Presbyterianism. Since this debate centers in theology rather than practice, it also signals a shift in concern from Sabbath observance to Sabbath doctrine, especially the doctrine of the Sunday Sabbath. Hence the Dedham debate represents the critical turning point in the sixteenth-century history of the English Sabbath.[4]

At the very first meeting of the Dedham conference on 3 December 1582, "the question touching the right use of the lord's day" was raised.[5] Subsequently, the issue surfaced twelve times during the next four years. The last mention of the Sabbath issue is at the meeting on 3 January 1586. The minutes reflect much debate but very little progress toward a solution. The entry for 4 February 1583 is typical: "The question of the use of the Sabbath was then debated of but left undetermined till further conference of brethren in other places might be required." There is no reference to the results of such quests for enlightenment from other places.

At the meeting of 24 June 1583 "it was agreed on that the Question of the Sabbath before propounded should carefully be considered of and every man give his reasons to D. Crick and he to answer them at the next meeting, and that Mr. D. Chapman, Mr. Stockton and Mr. Morse crave the judgements of some godly men in Cambridge touching the question of the Sabbath." The central issues of concern were also defined at this meeting. "The state of the question is this first, that there is a Sabbath. 2) It is not a whole natural day. 3) That we be not bound to the same rest that was with the Jews."

The debate intensified later in 1583 and in the spring of 1584. It is apparent from the minutes that the two protagonists were Richard Crick and Henry Sandes.[6] Crick was the only Oxford-educated member of

---

[4]Curiously, previous studies of the English Sabbath have not discussed this debate in detail in spite of its historical significance. Kenneth Parker deals with the Dedham debate only briefly and later describes the debated issues as "peripheral." *The English Sabbath*, 165ff., 222.

[5]Where minutes are identified by date, footnote page references are not given.

[6]Minutes of 24 June, 5 August, 7 October 1583; 13 January, 6 April, and 1 June 1584. Usher includes very brief sketches of the ministers involved in the classical movement. *The Presbyterian Movement*, xxxvff.

the Dedham conference. Although he took what might in retrospect be described as a non-Puritan position on the Sabbath, no conclusions should be drawn about his Oxford training, for he had been a fellow at Magdalen, the college Collinson describes as "perhaps the most re-markable puritan society in either university."[7] Crick was, moreover, quite actively involved in the presbyterian movement and had run afoul of ecclesiastical authorities already in 1573 for his outspoken support of Thomas Cartwright. He had been one of the leaders of a presbyte-rian experiment in Norwich and was one of the founders of the Ded-ham conference. Very little is known about Henry Sandes, except that he was a pastor at Boxford near Dedham.

At the meeting on 7 October 1583, conference time was spent "ex-amining Mr. D. Crick's travails about that question [concerning the Sabbath]." Crick had apparently been appointed as a committee of one to research the Sabbath matter. Every member, however, was encour-aged to "bring in his reasons for the right use of the sabbath." The minutes of 13 January 1584 report that "Mr. Sandes alleged some rea-sons against Mr. D. Crick's labors about the Sabbath which were to be brought in writing the next meeting." On 6 April "Mr. Sandes brought in his reasons against Mr. D. Crick's labors about the sabbath; it was thought good Mr. D. should have them and answer them at the next meeting." This was apparently done at the May meeting, for the min-utes of 1 June 1584 indicate that Sandes was absent and hence did not reply to Crick's response.

The two position papers by Sandes and Crick have been preserved in the collection of papers and letters appended to the Dedham min-utes. The first one is apparently Sandes's response to Crick's "labors about the sabbath" alluded to in the 6 April minutes. The second is Crick's much lengthier rebuttal of Sandes's position, filled with quo-tations of specific statements made by Sandes. Sandes's arguments are brief and somewhat sketchy, suggesting that he may have been re-sponding to arguments orally delivered by Crick in the discussion ses-sions of some earlier Dedham meetings. While we are at some disadvantage in not having access to the original arguments to which Sandes is responding, it is not difficult to discern the chief differences that arose within this Dedham company of pastors.

---

[7]Collinson, *The Elizabethan Puritan Movement*, 129.

Essentially the three topics cited in the minutes of 24 June 1583 are addressed in these papers. First, the question of the *day*. Is the first day of the week sacrosanct? Is that day set aside for worship and rest by divine command or is it simply a matter of church tradition? Is Sunday the New Testament Sabbath? In the closing decades of the sixteenth century, this became the issue of fundamental, definitive importance in Sabbatarianism. There is sharp disagreement between Sandes and Crick on this basic issue. Sandes begins, "That there is a Sabbath I do also freely confess. That the church is at liberty to change the day, although I profess myself ready to be informed yet methinks that which is said doth not satisfy me."[8] Apparently, both of the disputants agree that there is a Sabbath—that the Old Testament Sabbath of the fourth commandment continues into the New Testament era and on into the sixteenth century. But they disagree about whether the church is bound by some kind of divine precept to observe the Sabbath on a particular day, namely, the first day of the week. Although the fundamental issue is that of the day, it is significant that that issue is entered by way of the question concerning the church's liberty to change the day. There is no indication that the ecclesiastical authorities ever considered changing the day. And yet, in the highly charged atmosphere of the presbyterian challenge to episcopal government, it was an urgent question nonetheless.

Before establishing his convictions about the nature of the first-day Sabbath itself, Sandes continues with some comment about church policies that exist by divine right. He states that "many things in the policy of the church there be which it is not in man's power to alter, as the general matter of the government, etc., by this except I be deceived, we throw ourselves down before the adversaries of the church government."[9]

This allusion to "the adversaries of the church government" is puzzling; at first blush it would seem that the presbyterians themselves were the chief adversaries of the government of the established church. But Sandes has something else in mind, and the matter is clarified in

[8]Rylands English MS 874 fol. 237a.

[9]Ibid.

Crick's rebuttal. Crick identifies the "adversaries of church government" as those "against whom we maintained the general matter of
government is an essential part of a reformed church, and not a matter
of mere policy and order."[10] Both Crick and Sandes, indeed the entire
Dedham conference, were sympathetic with the presbyterian movement and its insistence that a truly Reformed church must have a truly
Reformed government. Sandes fears that to place the time of the Sabbath within the church's jurisdiction—hence making it a matter of
"mere policy and order"—would ultimately be a concession to the
episcopal system. Very early in this Dedham debate, therefore, an explicit connection is made between developing Sabbatarian convictions
and the controversy over church government. Those Sabbatarian convictions are, at least in part, to be accounted for in terms of political
bias against the current administrators of the church. On the other
hand, the existence of dispute over the Sabbath among the Dedham
Puritans indicates that not all, at least not Richard Crick, were allowing their politics to shape their Sabbath theology.

The argument then turns to the nature of the Sabbath commandment itself, a critical issue in the debate over the church's power to alter the day. Is it a "moral" or "ceremonial" law? The moral law is
creational, embedded in the unchangeable fabric of the universe, perpetual and relevant for all people at all times. Ceremonial laws are peculiar to Old Testament Israel—not universal but restricted to time and
place, given to guide the religious life of the ancient Israelites, and later
fulfilled by Christ.

If the Sabbath commandment is ceremonial, then it need not be observed by the New Testament church and the decision regarding the
time of worship becomes the church's prerogative. If, however, the
fourth commandment is part of the moral law, then the church's authority is drastically qualified vis-à-vis the Sabbath and its observance.
Sandes adopts the prevailing view that there are both ceremonial and
moral dimensions in the Sabbath commandment. There is "some ceremony" in it but also "perpetual policy."[11] For biblical support, Sandes
appeals to the practice of the apostles in the New Testament. Since they

[10]Ibid., fol. 242a.
[11]Ibid., fol. 237a.

observed the Sabbath (even though it was on the first day of the week), it is certain that the Old Testament Sabbath was not purely and exclusively ceremonial. Sandes even concedes that not all apostolic practices were "perpetual," but argues that some were and then simply declares the Sabbath as one of them. The burden of proof, he believes, lies on those who wish to contend that "this is one of them that were not perpetual." Sandes insists that Sunday worship is not merely instituted and initiated by the church, "but came from heaven and therefore is more weighty."[12]

Richard Crick, in his rebuttal, is convinced that in the Scriptures "nothing concerning a settled 7th day was commanded," at least not in the New Testament. If Crick is right, Sandes is placed in the uncomfortable position of showing "that the church is necessarily tied unto that whereof ye have no commandment from the Lord." Furthermore, if the fourth commandment with respect to the Sabbath day is not only ceremonial but moral also, "then the day could not have been changed unto another," that is, from the seventh to the first.[13]

In the exchange on the issue of apostolic institution as an argument for the perpetual relevance of the Sabbath in the New Testament church, the scholastic style of the debate is clearly illustrated. Sandes argues: "As the objection doth not hold that every apostolic institution is perpetual, so methinks the answer is not sufficient except it were showed that this is one of them that were not perpetual. But for that which is added, of doing without conference, it maketh for the authority of the thing that it was not a church conclusion but came from heaven and therefore is more weighty."[14] To this, Crick gives a lengthy reply, beginning with an allusion to Sandes's statement, "except it were showed that this is one of the scriptural institutions that were not perpetual." This, says Crick,

> hath no ground, for why should I show that here which was not avouched by the objection, and it is alone as if you had said that my answer is insufficient, except I should grant that which I deny, for if I show that this is one of the apostolic institutions which is not perpetual, I grant

---

[12]Ibid., fol. 237b.

[13]Ibid., fol. 242a.

[14]Ibid., fol. 237b.

it to be an institution of theirs, which being the assumption in the argument is denied of me. Neither doth it suffice for the proving of it to be one, that it was used in some places, no more than the assembling together of the church in Jerusalem every day in the week doth prove it to be an apostolic institution that we should assemble every day in the week.[15]

The discussion then turns to the question of whether, in this New Testament era, it is still necessary to tie the church to a particular day for its Sabbath. Sandes argues that "if Adam in his innocence" had need of such a day, the Sabbath having been established as a creational ordinance, then we have not less but much more need of it today. This is not only because of the Fall, which has made us "far inferior to him in all things," but also because there are so many redemptive matters that the first-day Sabbath holds before our attention, especially the Resurrection. Sandes describes the Resurrection as "the official accomplishment of our re-creation."[16] This allusion to redemption as re-creation, implicitly linking the doctrines of Resurrection and Creation, hints of a theological tendency of considerable importance in English Calvinism.

To maintain a Sabbath in our time, Sandes suggests, is not simply to revive an ancient Jewish ceremony. Rather, the New Testament Sabbath is uniquely and qualitatively different because it is tied to the Resurrection. It is "the lord's day," for the apostles themselves put "his special name" upon it. And since 1 Corinthians 16:1 specifies "in plain words" that it is to be held on "the first day of the week," we have a biblical institution "leaving then no liberty herein." We have, moreover, in the observance of the Sabbath on the first day of the week a practice that the church has never "been bold to break, no not even the papists which have transposed all things." So the theological argument relative to the day returns to the practical issue—the freedom and authority of the church relative to the Sabbath. Sandes concludes with this clincher: "Further when it hath his name, the lord's day, I think it is of his authority in commanding it and severing it from the rest, which if it be so . . . I see not how any man may alter it."[17]

[15]Ibid., fol. 242b.

[16]Ibid., fol. 237b.

[17]Ibid., fol. 238b.

The rebuttal becomes particularly testy in its response to the claim that the church has always been content with a first-day Sabbath. After suggesting that the protestant churches have made some changes in the traditional medieval Catholic observances of such Sundays as Easter and Pentecost, Crick goes on to declare: "but what proof is there that it hath not been changed at any time but that every church hath retained it and held it? I will show some reason why I think that it hath been changed. Constantine the great made a law for the celebrating of that day on the first of the week as it is manifest out of Sozemenus which statute of his being made unto the church, is most likely to have had ground from their using of another day."[18] Then he appeals to Henry Bullinger, who refers also to this act of Constantine and comments that the emperor here "renewed the custom of the Apostles." If the custom was said to be "renewed," it must have been a custom that was "almost worn out for if it had been commonly used, how might it well be said to be renewed? If it were fresh in use what need for any renovation?"[19]

The rebuttal focuses on Sandes's use of an adjective to modify "church" when he argues that no "particular church" may change the Lord's day. Crick uses this as the occasion to launch into a lengthy and involved argument regarding his basic position on the rights of the church.

And it seemeth unto me by your word that the universal church may change it for if you mean not so, why did you not rather say the church than limit it by adding the word particular: which if you grant me, I gain my question, which is not whether it may be changed by this or that church but whether it may be changed at all, yea that being afforded me, it will follow first that it is no commandment of the apostles which you set down seeing the church hath no more power to change any precept then to turn the day into night. Secondly that a particular church may change it for herself, which I prove by this argument: that which the universal church may do for herself generally in a council ecumenical, the same may a particular church, national or provincial, do for herself, particularly in a national or provincial council, for a particular church hath as much authority to take a particular order for her own private as the whole hath to take a common order for the whole. If

[18]Ibid., fol. 243b.

[19]Ibid.

therefore that be granted which I gather by your word, it falleth out that even a church of a nation or province might change it if occasion served.[20]

The second main topic in this Sabbath debate concerns the length of the day. The real issue here is whether the Sabbath should be understood and observed in terms of a "natural day," or whether as the New Testament fulfillment of an Old Testament type it should be seen as a "figurative day" with a figurative rest. Both agree the Old Testament Sabbath was a natural day. Sandes indicates their agreement as well as their disagreement in his opening statement: "That the Jews' Sabbath was a natural day I do like very well, but that ours should not be methinks I yet do not see."[21] His appeal is again to the creational origin of the Sabbath when he says, "Again when it was thus long afore the ceremonies for the rudeness of the church and that burden of Moses was instituted, I see not how the length of it should be shut up in a ceremony."[22]

Sandes follows with five brief statements of rebuttal to points made by his opponent in the original presentation. These points are made so tersely, however, that it is very difficult to reconstruct the original argument. The Crick rebuttal at this point, though much more extensive, is somewhat abstruse. A persistent tactic that he employs is to push Sandes into an extreme literalness that leads to the absurd. If Sandes wants to speak of a natural, literal day, then he must espouse natural, literal rest on that day. Crick calls attention to the plain words of the commandment forbidding any work "even unto the gathering of a few sticks or kindling of a fire, or dressing a piece of meat."[23] Sandes had argued, on the other hand, that on the Sabbath not all labor is forbidden but rather the "ill use" of it.[24]

To this Crick responds with a long argument beautifully illustrating how well he had learned his logic lessons in the scholastic curriculum. He states,

---

[20]Ibid., fol. 244a.

[21]Ibid., fol. 238b.

[22]Ibid.

[23]Ibid., fol. 244b.

[24]Ibid., fol. 239a.

Now to that no more than in the rest of the commandments the things are not in all their kind forbidden, but such ill use of them, I answer first nothing is forbidden in any of the commandments whereof all the kind are not forbidden, for if the general, then also all the special contained under it. And if any of the specials comprehended underneath the special be expressed, then the general is not prohibited: as if dishonoring of parents and adultery be unlawful generally, then can there not be found one kind of them allowable. Secondly, in saying (but such ill use of them) you insinuate some good use of the things forbidden, now whereas nothing is forbidden but sin, it followeth that there is some good use of sin.[25]

We have seen that Sandes's arguments frequently turn to the early, creational beginning or institution of a Sabbath day. Here again, his reasons for considering the Sabbath a natural day all center in its creational origin, which proves that it is no mere Mosaic ceremony. He writes, "That order is to be kept which was afore any ceremony (as we do speak of them) was, or the rudeness of the church required any such thing."[26]

In his rebuttal Crick exploits the obvious flaw. If we are bound by the creation order, then we are bound to a *seventh-day* Sabbath. "If you mean simply whatsoever you speak for a natural day I will hence speak for the very seventh day, for if the being of the order before shall be the cause of keeping the order still, then the being of the seventh day before shall be the cause of keeping the seventh day."[27]

As an additional reason why we should regard the Sabbath as a natural day, Sandes again refers to the example of Adam in paradise. For "if Adam had need of so much time (i.e., a natural day of 24 hours) being in far better state than we are, for meditation of the creation, we have need rather of more than of less."[28] The rebuttal seeks to lay this argument to rest once and for all.

Now the truth is that at the beginning the church needed ceremonies, for what were the tree of life and the tree of knowledge of good and evil but ceremonies? And what was that seventh day but a ceremony? If

---

[25]Ibid., fol. 244b.

[26]Ibid., fol. 239a.

[27]Ibid., fol. 245a.

[28]Ibid., fol. 239b.

Adam did not need them wherefore did the Lord appoint them being superfluous? And so I come to answer your reason, which is that if Adam needed 24 hours we need them much more, for by the same reason it may be said, that if Adam needed those ceremonies we need them much more. But the truth is that we can no more say, If he had need of that then we much more, then we can say, If Abraham had need of circumcision then we have more need of circumcision, or if the Jews had need of many feast days, then we have much more, the reason whereof is for that it was a ceremony appointed for him in that time. Now although in the thesis the reason be good, if Adam needed a ceremony to help him we much more, yet it followeth not in the hypothesis that if he needed this therefore we need the same, seeing the Lord hath provided us of more excellent and more significant. And therefore if it should be granted that we have more need, it followeth not thereof that we must hold that rate of time for if because we have more need of 24 hours than he, therefore we be bound to hold 24 hours, then because we have more need of fourscore hours than he had of 24 we be bound to hold 4 score and because we have more need of 10 sacraments than he had of two (our faith being weaker and we having ten times greater matters to be put in mind of) therefore we be bound to have ten. But I do deny that we have more need being otherwise provided for, and by this which is said, I think that is answered which was alleged of Adam for the resurrection day.[29]

The third Sabbath issue addressed in the record of the Dedham discussions pertains to the nature of the rest on that day and the interrelated matter of the proper activities or "busyness" of the Sabbath. Sandes's opening statement indicates that once again there is both agreement and disagreement: "That we be not bound to the straight order of rest that they were, for the substantial part I do like of that, as say public meetings, but I do not yet think that this is all the work of the sabbath."[30] Again, the ceremonial versus the moral character of the fourth commandment is the underlying issue. Sandes agrees that there are "ceremonial appendices" to the Sabbath commandment but when the Sabbath is called a sign, this does not indicate the Old Testament ceremony should be ignored. Sandes writes: "For by being a sign I cannot see how any other thing could be meant but a common token that the Lord by this calling them from their common busyness to hear

---

[29]Ibid., fol. 245b.

[30]Ibid., fol. 239b.

his word and to be exercised especially this way, doth beckon to them that it is he that must work their sanctification, as by forbidding murder it is a sign that the life of man is dear unto him, and therefore the word here doth not signify any type but a common sign as Tremelius also speaketh of it. Exodus 31."[31] Sandes argues that the "principal end" for which God instituted the Sabbath was not to provide a type or sign for Israel that would find its fulfillment in Christ. Rather, "the end why it was commanded is that his word might be heard and his spirit more effectually work in them and as for hearing the word and weighing it though it be not all the business yet is it more especially enjoined that day than any other and must have more special time allowed to it."[32]

The lengthy rebuttal of these arguments includes a number of indications that Crick's fundamental understanding of the Sabbath is that of an Old Testament ceremony: "I persuade myself the Sabbath was such a sign unto them, as others so-called were, a seal of blessings and good things promised as the rainbow that sealed up to Noah that the world should no more be drowned with water. And as circumcision which sealed unto Abraham that God was his god and he with his seed his people . . . whereby it appeareth that it is not called a sign because it is a commandment as you speak, but because it carried a lowly representation of some good thing to come by Christ Jesus which was sanctification."[33]

The different emphases on the ceremonial and moral understandings of the Sabbath result in separate views about appropriate punishment. Sandes believes Sabbath breaking may be coercively, civilly punished just as is blasphemy. Crick responds that because "the precise rest of the day was ceremonial, the punishment cannot be brought into the commonwealth,"[34] suggesting that the punishments prescribed by the Old Testament are inappropriate for sixteenth-century civil order.

Concluding the discussion is a long and complex argument about the meaning of the Matthew 12 pericope relating Jesus' defense of the

---

[31]Ibid., fols. 239b, 240a.

[32]Ibid , fol. 240a.

[33]Ibid., fol. 246a.

[34]Ibid., fol. 246b.

disciples' picking corn on the Sabbath. Much of the argument turns on whether the "sabbath" in this story is the true biblical Sabbath that God instituted, or whether it is a sabbath of the Pharisees' own devising. The argument becomes quite sophisticated, including comparison of the three synoptic accounts, the precise meaning of a number of Greek terms, and appeal to other biblical authorities.

The Dedham papers demonstrate that the Sabbath issue had become a subject for lively debate in the Church of England by the early 1580s. The Dedham conference was organized as a forum for discussion of mutual problems that the clergy in Essex encountered in their parishes. There is no issue that comes up more frequently during the brief life span of the conference than the issue of the Sabbath. Earlier, as we have seen, there had been a consensus in England regarding the Sabbath. High Sabbath views were reflected in many of the writings of the leading reformers and even make their way into the official book of homilies published with the blessing of the queen and archbishop. The Dedham papers on the Sabbath, however, indicate that a serious disagreement with potentially explosive ramifications was threatening that consensus. It was a disagreement about the day, about whether by divine authority Sunday became our New Testament Sabbath. Prior to the 1580s, there is no indication that this was an especially significant issue. The idea of Sunday absolutism had been proposed in England already in 1548 by John Hooper, but his view had received little attention and debate.[35] In the 1580s, however, in the context of special concern about the extent of the church's authority, this doctrine gained new importance.

The Dedham debate also illustrates a new development in the content of the Sabbath discussions of the 1580s: a shift of emphasis from Sabbath observance to Sabbath theology. In the 1570s, the tracts and treatises of Humphrey Roberts, John Northbrooke, John Stockwood, and others contained concerns primarily about proper Sabbath observance, complaints about Sabbath abuse, and threats regarding God's vengeance against Sabbath breakers. This literature includes minimal theological discussion, probably because of an assumed consensus

---

[35]See above, 20-23.

about the basic doctrines regarding the Sabbath. The Dedham minutes indicate that the discussions there were also precipitated by practical questions about Sabbath observance that had arisen in the everyday life of the parish. But the two position papers analyzed here show that the practical questions led to, and then became obscured by, a re-examination of the theological underpinnings. The two papers of Sandes and Crick, in fact, deal very little with practical questions of Sabbath observance. They focus on the theology of the Sabbath and include tightly argued analyses of biblical data. This biblical-theological re-examination is a special feature of English Sabbath development in the last two decades of the sixteenth century. This new emphasis on Sabbath theology opened up the possibility of new directions in Sabbath understanding, but also, of course, the possibility of a gradual breakdown in the long-standing consensus.

The Dedham debate also suggests a connection between Sabbatarianism and Presbyterianism, giving more credibility to the Rogers-Heylyn interpretation than Kenneth Parker allows.[36] The opening paragraphs of Sandes's paper indicate that the question with which he enters deeper exploration of the meaning and theology of the Sabbath is whether the church has the authority and freedom to change the day from the first day of the week to some other at the church's convenience. Since there is no evidence that the church was remotely considering a change in the day of worship, why should this question arise at all? It is understandable only in terms of the highly charged ecclesiastical-political atmosphere of that time resulting from the presbyterian challenge to the church. The Dedham conference itself is a primary source of evidence for a developing, growing presbyterian movement in the church, a movement especially associated earlier in the 1570s with the name of Thomas Cartwright. Cartwright and others called for a fundamental change in the government of the Church of England, a change from an episcopal, hierarchical form of rule by "high clergy" and monarchy, to government that called for parity of clergy and greater local control of the church.

In such an atmosphere, it is not surprising to find these disputants over the Sabbath entering the debate with a question about the extent of the church's authority. Although the two papers eventually depart

---

[36]See above, 2-4.

from the issue of the church's authority to regulate the day of worship,
it is possible to interpret much of this Sabbath debate against the background of the church-government question. We should not minimize
the importance of that issue in eventual decisions about which side to
take on the Sabbath question. Although in the 1580s the lines were not
yet clearly and consistently drawn between Low Church Presbyterians and Sabbatarians, and High Church Anglicans and anti-Sabbatarians, the Dedham debate was a portent of things to come in the
following century.

Finally, the Dedham papers clearly demonstrate that in the early
1580s there was neither a Puritan nor Anglican mind on the Sabbath.
Initially, when the consensus on the Sabbath began to develop fis-
sures, it is historically inappropriate to describe the disagreements in
Puritan versus Anglican terms. Assuming the position papers on the
Sabbath were internally produced by clerical members of the Dedham
conference, it is apparent that there were sharp conflicts of opinion and
understanding of fundamental questions dealing with the character of
the Sabbath among the Puritan members of the conference itself. They
disagreed about the nature of the fourth commandment, especially
about the degree to which it was to be regarded as moral rather than
ceremonial. There was dispute about such matters as the length of the
day and the kind of rest the New Testament church should promote.
They argued about the extent of the church's authority in relation to
control of the day and its observance. It is tempting to analyze English
Protestantism in this period in terms of a sharp Puritan–Anglican division, but the lines of conflict are fuzzy and blurred.[37] In fact, the ministers of the Dedham conference were loyal Church of England
clergymen with probably no intentions of ever forsaking that Church.
They were "Anglicans" with moderate Puritan sympathies.

Although Puritans and Anglicans could not yet be distinguished in
the 1580s by means of their respective positions on the Sabbath, the
Dedham papers provide the first clear indication that problems about

[37]Much has been written on the appropriateness of these terms—especially
of the term *anglican*—as useful descriptions of the ecclesiastical situation in the
sixteenth century. The definition of Anglicanism is becoming as problematic
as the definition of Puritanism. See especially Peter Lake, *Anglicans and Puritans?* (London: Unwin Hyman, 1988).

the Sabbath were beginning to surface. A debate had begun, one that would lead to a new spate of Sabbath treatises and fourth commandment studies culminating in the full-blown Sabbatarianism of Nicholas Bound in 1595. Given the Establishment's concern about the presbyterian movement, it was inevitable that in the growing dispute about the underlying authority for a Sunday Sabbath, the drawn battle lines would place Puritan-Presbyterians on one side and Anglicans on the other.

3

THE
CAMBRIDGE CIRCLE

IN JUNE 1583, the ministers of the Dedham conference decided to go for help to settle their Sabbath dispute. Cambridge was only sixty miles away and possessed a veritable brain trust of earnest reformers who were at least moderate Puritans, "godly men" like Edward Dering, Thomas Cartwright, Laurence Chaderton, William Perkins, John Knewstubb, Richard Greenham, John Dod, and a host of others. St. John's, Trinity, Christ's and Emmanuel colleges contributed immensely to the rise and development of a Protestantism in England that had more than a tinge of Puritanism. At Cambridge interest in Decalogue study was at its peak in the 1580s, and in this context the fourth commandment received heavy attention.[1] So the Dedham ministers decided to secure "the judgements of some godly men in Cambridge touching the question of the Sabbath."[2]

[1]Gervase Babington's *Very Fruitful Exposition of the Commandements by Way of Questions and Answers* (London, 1583) was one of the first Decalogue studies to appear in the later decades of the century, but Lancelot Andrewes's lectures at Pembroke preceded Babington's publication. Cf. James Dennison, *The Market Day of the Soul* (Lanham MD: University Press of America, 1983) 29.

[2]Dedham minutes, 24 June 1583, eighth meeting. Cf. Roland G. Usher, *The Presbyterian Movement in the Reign of Queen Elizabeth* (London: Royal Historical Society, 1905) 30.

More than likely, some of these Dedham pastors had heard Lancelot Andrewes's lectures on the fourth commandment in the late 1570s. Andrewes matriculated at Pembroke College in 1571. In 1578 he was appointed the catechist of the college, a position that made him responsible for delivering weekend lectures on the faith. At three o'clock on Saturday and Sunday afternoons he lectured to large audiences. By all accounts he was a gifted theologian and an able speaker, and auditors "not only out of other colleges in the University, but divers also out of the country, did duly resort unto the college chapel" to hear him.[3]

Andrewes's lectures on the fourth commandment represent the beginning of another stage in the development toward full Sabbatarianism, a stage of much more extensive and detailed interpretation of the Sabbath commandment.[4] His lectures appear to have been the first extensive public articulation and theological defense of the high Sabbath views that had long been assumed and accepted in English Prot-

---

[3]H. Isaacson, *An Exact Narrative of the Life and Death of Lancelot Andrewes* (London: John Hearne, 1829) 29. Cf. Paul A. Welsby, *Lancelot Andrewes* (London: S. P. C. K., 1958); Trevor Owen, *Lancelot Andrewes* (Boston: Twayne, 1981).

[4]Andrewes himself did not publish these lectures. We are largely dependent on student notes handed down until they were first published in crude form in 1630 under the title *A Patterne of Catechisticall Doctrine*. This was reissued in 1641. In 1642 a much expanded version was published under the title *The Moral Law Expounded*. In 1650 an anonymous editor published a still fuller version, this time under the original title. If we can take the editor at his word, this is the best of the various editions, for he states in the preface, "Here is presented the Author's own Copy . . . being the only Copy he had, as is acknowledged under his hand in the beginning of the Book, and containing many Marginal Notes, and alterations throughout the whole made by himself in his latter years."

M. M. Knappen believes that with regard to the exposition of the fourth commandment, the 1642 edition is the most reliable, since the "Anglican editor" of the 1650 edition "altered" Andrewes's interpretation of the Sabbath. "The Early Puritanism of Lancelot Andrewes," *Church History* 2 (1933):101. A careful comparison of the two editions, however, reveals that although the text of the 1650 edition is expanded and much improved in terms of readability, it is in no respect "altered" in a more Anglican direction. The editor does add some explanatory notes and even an additional chapter of his own, but he clearly distinguishes his own work from that of Andrewes. The references that follow are from the 1650 edition reprinted in the Anglo Catholic Library, *Pattern of Catechistical Doctrine* (Oxford: Parker, 1846).

estantism. In an era when public lectures could indeed spark long, hot controversies, there is no evidence that his views stimulated any negative reaction. He does not state his case in as inflammatory a fashion as Nicholas Bound would a few years later. His style is that of the academic, full of appeal to the ancients, liberally studded with Latin quotations, and with a heavy dependence on Ramist principles of logic. He delivered lectures, not homilies, neither strident nor polemic in tone, but cool, straightforward analyses of the meaning and significance of the fourth commandment.

In several ways Andrewes nudges the Sabbath along toward a more highly developed Sabbatarianism. For example, he stresses the uniqueness of the fourth commandment among the commandments.[5] He finds a half-dozen ways in which this commandment differs from all the others. The upshot of the argument raises the status of the Sabbath command. In these final decades of the century there seemed to be an irresistible temptation to exalt the fourth commandment over the others. This tendency can be seen and understood in the larger context of the godly leaders' strong conviction that the only way to genuine and complete reformation was through the faithful ministry of the Word of God to all the people of England—a task best accomplished through weekly Sunday worship. Lancelot Andrewes shared in and contributed to this conviction.

Andrewes is also more emphatic regarding the creation origin of the Sabbath command than any previous author. He states that the command originated in God's own pattern of work and rest in the creation of the world. Adam first received this commandment "in the state of innocency." Even in his sinless condition he needed a day for "spiritual use and consideration."[6] And if Adam needed that in a state of perfection, how much more we need our Sabbath in our sinful condition. Andrewes develops the familiar emphasis on the moral character of the fourth commandment with no less than six reasons to support the continuing binding character of the law of the Sabbath. It was given to remind mankind of God's creation of the world, and it is this "continuing of the memory of the creation" that keeps mankind from pa-

---

[5]Ibid., 260.

[6]Ibid., 263, 265.

ganism and "atheism."[7] The creation purpose is more pronounced for Andrewes than the redemptive purpose of the Sabbath which he views as "accessory," added only as a result of the Fall.

In his discussion of the change of day from the seventh to the first, Andrewes argues that no day of the week is by nature any holier than any other. Yet "God's ordinance, by separating one day from another for himself, makes it to be more holy than the rest."[8] The change of day comes to us with the weight of apostolic authority, and he seems to equate Sunday with the Jewish Sabbath. "But it is manifest, that instead of the Jews' seventh day, another seventh day was ordained in the Apostles' days."[9] As the seals of the covenant were changed from circumcision and Passover to baptism and Lord's Supper, so the "Day of the Covenant" was changed by the Apostles from the seventh to the first. This sort of parallelism gives considerable weight to Sunday as *the* day of worship. Andrewes does not explicitly address the issue of the church's authority to change the day, but his argument about the change leaves the clear impression that it took place by divine right and was not simply an ecclesiastical tradition. The reason for the selection of the first day of the week is related to the events of Resurrection and Pentecost, both occurring on the first day of the week. This does not mean that the original end of creation remembrance has been laid aside, for "the memory of the benefit of creation may also be kept on the first day of the week as well as on the last."[10] But now the day has trinitarian significance. "Hence we may see upon what great reasons this day is established, wherein do concur the three special works and benefits of the three persons to be forever thankfully remembered, namely that of creation by the Father, redemption by the Son, and sanctification by the Holy Ghost."[11]

Andrewes's views on proper Sabbath observance are very stringent. He finds six prohibitions limiting Sabbath activity in the Scriptures, and implies that they still have bearing on our use of Sunday

[7]Ibid., 280.

[8]Ibid., 261.

[9]Ibid., 267.

[10]Ibid.

[11]Ibid.

today. He concludes with the observation that "the Prophets generally urge the observation of this commandment above the rest."[12] He does not comment extensively on the problem of recreation on the Sabbath, but does mention at one point that "the desire we have after sports and pastimes" is a common impediment.[13] Later he calls a Sabbath spent with plays, dancing, hunting, dicing, carding, and feasting as "the Sabbath of the golden calf."[14]

More positively, Andrewes enumerates the duties to be carried out on the Sabbath: prayer, public worship, meditation, conversation or "conference," thanksgiving and praise, and works of mercy. Emphasis on works of mercy is especially pronounced in Andrewes. God delights in nothing more than deeds of mercy toward the needy. He observes that there is a "special affinity betwixt sanctification of the day and work of mercy," which includes both material care for the poor and needy, and spiritual care such as teaching, comfort, reproof, prayer, and personal reconciliation.[15]

When measured by his later career as a respected, faithful bishop, Andrewes does not appear to be a likely Sabbatarian. After the turn of the century, he became bishop of Chichester, later of Ely, and finally of Winchester until his death in 1626. In his earlier years, especially at Cambridge, Andrewes seemed to be in sympathy with the Puritan promoters of more advanced reform in the church. But instead of debating whether Andrewes was a Puritan or Anglican, we should see him as another reminder that party lines may not be forced upon this period of English Reformation history. He also illustrates that Puritanism and Sabbatarianism were hardly exceptions to the rule at this time.[16]

---

[12]Ibid., 282.

[13]Ibid., 337.

[14]Ibid., 343.

[15]Ibid., 291, 292.

[16]Welsby, *Lancelot Andrewes*, 118. About Andrewes's Sabbath views Welsby says, "It is but another example that on this matter Puritanism and a large body of Anglicanism were at one."

More than anyone else, Richard Greenham deserves the title "patriarch of English Sabbatarianism." He was an older friend and spiritual mentor of Andrewes. Earlier he had been, like Andrewes, a fellow at Pembroke College, and in 1570 he became rector of the parish church at Dry Drayton, near Cambridge. There he spent more than two decades, from 1570 to 1591, as preacher and pastor.[17]

Greenham could well be used as a prototype for what has come to be known as "moderate Puritanism" in the sixteenth-century Church of England, a spirit somewhat restless and ill at ease with conditions in the church and dissatisfied with the progress of reform, yet essentially peace-loving and loyal to established authority. Greenham had much contact with Cambridge students, and Henry Holland, the editor of his works, stated that he had a restraining influence, keeping many from "schism and error, striving always to retain such in obedience of laws and preciously to esteem and regard the peace of the Church and people of God."[18] A loyal subject of the monarch, he "much rejoiced and praised God for the happy government of our most gracious Queen Elizabeth."[19]

It is in the context of his role as a moderate Puritan, dedicated parish minister, warmly sympathetic pastor, and godly preacher that Greenham's treatise on the Sabbath must be read and appreciated. Although it did not appear in published form until the early 1590s, it is undoubtedly based upon convictions that had been fully developed earlier in Cambridge and were regularly proclaimed from his Dry Drayton pulpit. The treatise begins like a sermon: "Dearly beloved in the Lord, there is no commandment of God's part more urged, and of our parts less observed, than this one of the Sabbath."[20]

If Nicholas Bound be our norm, perhaps Richard Greenham was not quite a full-blown Sabbatarian, but he was very nearly so. The

---

[17]John B. Marsden, *The History of the Early Puritans* (London: Hamilton, Adams, and Co., 1850) 240, 241. On Richard Greenham see *Dictionary of National Biography*, and Samuel Clarke, *The Lives of Thirty-two English Divines* (London, 1677).

[18]Richard Greenham, *The Works of the Reverend and Faithful Servant of Jesus Christ M. Richard Greenham*, ed. Henry Holland (London, 1599) fol. A5.

[19]Ibid., 14.

[20]Greenham, *Works*, 300.

fourth commandment receives elevated stature when he says, "in the book of God, when the Lord will urge the observation of the whole law, he often doth it under this one word of keeping the Sabbath." The heart and soul of his Sabbatarianism was essentially pastoral. He was convinced that the secret to a godly, spiritual, blessed life lay in the Sabbath institution and in its careful observance. "For seeing the Sabbath day is the school day, the fair day, the market day, the feeding day of the soul, when men purely knowing the use of it, separate it wholly from other days, they shall see how they may recover themselves from sins already past, arm themselves against sin to come, grow in knowledge, increase in faith, and how much they shall be strengthened in the inner man."[21] For Greenham the end and purpose of the Sabbath was nothing less than the pure worship of God, and true love of God and neighbor. That is why the fourth commandment is strategically positioned between the two tables of the law. Clearly he regards the fourth commandment as unique among the commandments.

Greenham takes one more step in the escalating emphasis on the creation origins of the Sabbath with the astonishing claim that this commandment alone was "in express words enjoined unto Adam and Eve in Paradise." Hence, "this one precept is the school of all the other commandments."[22] This, he believes, proves beyond any possible dispute that the fourth commandment is not essentially ceremonial. The Sabbath is rooted in the very nature of things, it is a created ordinance, part of the law embedded in the framework of the universe as God created it. So the Sabbath commandment has perpetual moral relevance. Greenham spells out the difference between moral and ceremonial, writing, "that I call moral, which doth inform man's manners either concerning their religion to God, or their duties unto man; that I mean figurative (or ceremonial), which is added for a time in some respect to some persons for an help to that which is moral."[23]

The Sabbath figures very prominently for Greenham in the covenant, serving a kind of mediatorial role between God and man as emphasized in Exodus 31 and Ezekiel 20. The Sabbath, he says, "is a

[21]Ibid., 301.

[22]Ibid., 306, 307.

[23]Ibid., 307.

document and pledge of God's will, whereby we should know, what he is unto us, and wherein we should learn what we should do to him."[24] Greenham explicitly rejects the idea that the Sabbath is simply and solely a sign of eternal, spiritual rest, although of course he also accepts that dimension of the Sabbath taught in the book of Hebrews. Throughout the English Sabbath literature, there is very little concern for this dimension, probably because it does not sufficiently lead to the immediate ethical implications of the Sabbath. The Sabbath is indeed an emblem of eternal rest, and the rest should be a "resting from sin." But this does not remove the need for a weekly day of rest from daily work for the purpose of worship and good works. We must rest "from the works of our callings and consequently from the works of sin much more."[25]

In a lengthy polemical section Greenham answers a number of objections to his view of the Sabbath, suggesting again that some disputes had arisen by the 1580s. Whether or not Greenham engaged in an internal struggle within the Church of England is uncertain. But it is more likely that his polemics are primarily directed toward opposition from the outside. At the beginning of the treatise he mentions his principal adversaries as papists on the one hand and Anabaptists on the other. Throughout the polemic section Greenham displays a broad knowledge of the Scriptures and a skillful handling of individual texts and passages. He is careful to take context into account and says "we must not stand upon the titles of letters, but observe the scope of the writer, and weigh the drift of the epistle."[26] This emphasis, along with his somewhat functional approach to the Sabbath, saves him from a rigid literalism. He defines a Sabbath day's journey, for example, as "that distance, as a man conveniently may travel for some holy purpose, without any hindrance of the ordinary exercise of that day, and without wearisomeness either to body or mind, whereby he should be the unfitter for the Lord's worship, or his duties."[27] The Sabbath rest does not mean cessation of all activity, but only of our "ordinary call-

---

[24]Ibid., 309.

[25]Ibid., 351.

[26]Ibid., 346.

[27]Ibid., 330.

ings." In fact, Greenham's vision for a proper Sabbath involves almost ceaseless activity, an emphasis that is apparent in nearly all successive Sabbatarian treatises.

On what would become the central Sabbatarian issue, that of the alteration of the day from the seventh to the first day of the week, Greenham begins cautiously: "It was never commanded nor appointed what one certain day should be kept among seven, but that there should be observed a seventh day: which being kept, it is sufficient, and the law remaineth unviolated." But he continues in a more definite Sabbatarian direction: "And yet we permit not, that any man at his pleasure should now change this day. For that which the Apostles did, they did not as private men, but as men guided by the spirit of God."[28]

Elsewhere in his *Works*, Greenham takes an even more precise Sabbatarian position on the shift to the first day of the week. He says, "That it should be changed once, it was meet, but never to be changed again, for as then the day of rest for the creation was most fit: so now the day of our redemption is most fit, seeing now the world is as if it were made new, and therefore cannot be changed."[29]

He concludes the discussion on alteration with the Trinitarian interpretation of the first day of the week: it is a fitting day because it was the first day of the creation of the world, it was the day of Christ's resurrection, and it was the day on which the Spirit was poured out. "So that this day doth fitly put us in mind of our creation to be thankful to God the Father, of our redemption to be thankful to God the Son, and of our sanctification to be thankful to God the Holy Ghost."[30]

According to Greenham Sabbath observance is centered in public worship. All else serves that end including the private acts of meditation, prayer, reflection, and discussion that should take place before, between, and after the public services. He urges public gatherings for worship in which the Word read and preached stands at the center at least twice each Sunday. Public exercises should also include prayer, psalm singing, and administration of the sacraments. To prepare for

---

[28]Ibid., 356.

[29]Greenham, *Works* (1612), 811.

[30]Greenham, *Works* (1599), 356.

public worship, participants must engage in the "stirring up" of themselves by conducting a personal inventory of blessings and sins. Just
as businessmen who "at least once in the week they search their books,
cast their accounts, confer with their gain their expenses, and make
even reckonings, whereby they may see whether they have gained, or
whether they have lost," so we must examine "how we have gone forward in godly proceedings, or how we have gone backward."[31] This
proper preparation, furthermore, begins with early rising, for "by
bathing our bodies in our beds on that day more than on any other . . .
we make it a day of our rest, and not of the Lord's rest."[32]

The strong ethical thrust of Greenham's Sabbath is reflected in his
admonitions about Sabbath observance between and after the services. Showing love to others is the fruit of the public service, for the
"Sabbath is not a day of knowledge alone, but of love; not only of hearing the word by preaching, but also of doing the word by practising."[33]
We must respond to the needs of our neighbors both in body and in
soul by visiting the sick and imprisoned, helping the poor and miserable, feeding the hungry, clothing the naked, comforting the distressed, bestowing our goods on the needy, and by witnessing,
teaching the ignorant, and bringing them to repentance. These private
exercises must also lead to greater personal sanctification in terms of
increased faith and repentance through the deeper application of the
public service through "reading [what was not clearly understood in
the sermon], comparing of things heard, examining and applying them
to ourselves, praying, thanksgiving, and meditating."[34]

For Greenham the Sabbath is the key to a full appreciation of the
Christian's new life in Christ. It is not a separate compartment for spiritual life, but the enabling mechanism to get all of life into proper perspective once again, for "as our callings serveth to God's worship, so
God's worship sanctifieth our callings."[35] "True it is," he writes, "that
this spiritual use and holy meditation of the creatures of God should

[31]Ibid., 359, 360.

[32]Ibid., 361.

[33]Ibid., 366.

[34]Ibid., 362.

[35]Ibid., 370.

be our whole life: howbeit because our distractions in our lawful and ordinary callings will not permit this so fully in respect of our finite nature, we must remember on the Sabbath day to use a recovery, and by Christian diligence to make recompense for our former negligence herein."[36] The Sabbath frees us from the cares of ordinary callings so that we may rest our bodies and refresh our spirits. In this sense the fourth commandment provides a means of grace.

Greenham enters into a detailed discussion of what is forbidden on the Sabbath, but he sets the tone of the discussion by stressing that "works are not simply forbidden, but so far forth as they be hindrances to the holy observation" of the Sabbath day.[37] Greenham avoids the legalism into which Sabbatarianism eventually fell by stressing the proper function and use of the day as the framework to discuss forbidden works. Most of the specifics he mentions are governed by the agricultural situation of his parish, and he takes a rather firm position on the need for Sabbath keeping also in times of harvest. As for "milking of kine, making of beds, and dressing of meats, as for travelers, bakers and brewers, . . . their business, if it be necessary, must be done either early in the morning, or lately in the evening."[38] On the Sabbath, otherwise lawful pleasures and recreations should be avoided, but again only by reason of their distracting us and impeding us from the proper sanctifying of the day. "And this we shall see more plainly, if we remember that rest is so far commanded, as it is an help and furtherance to sanctification, and labour so far is forbidden, as it is an impediment of the same. In regard whereof, if pleasures be no less lets and impediments to the hallowing of the Sabbath, than bodily and ordinary labours, then pleasures have no more liberty on the Lord's day than our outward works."[39]

So much has been made of the stringent restrictions of the Puritan Sabbath that it is surprising to find, when actually reading the Sabbath treatises, a positive tone and note of joy in them. The Sabbath for Greenham and others was really a day of freedom—freedom from or-

---

[36]Ibid., 364, 365.

[37]Ibid., 369.

[38]Ibid., 373.

[39]Ibid., 383.

dinary cares and callings, enabling God's people to rest their bodies
and refresh their souls. The Sabbath was a gift from God, designed to
play a key role in the Christian's sanctification. Disciplined use of the
day was therefore essential. Greenham urges that each Sabbath day
should end with an evening inventory.

> On this manner then we may expostulate with ourselves: Hath the Lord's
> increase of mercy brought me a day's increase of holiness? How is my
> knowledge increased, my affections touched, my faith strengthened, my
> repentance renewed, the love to the saints in me confirmed? How did
> the word prick my heart? How were my affections quickened by prayer?
> How much was my faith strengthened in the sacraments? Hath the Sab-
> bath been our delight? Are we nearer to God in faith and repentance?
> Are we nearer to our brethren in love and benevolence? Are we better
> affected to the glory of God? Is sin more grievous unto us, than it hath
> been? If it be, give God the glory in Christ.[40]

By all accounts, William Perkins was an extraordinarily gifted theologian, preacher, and teacher whose accomplishments were astonishing, especially for one whose entire life span was not quite forty-four
years. He was born in 1558, the first year of Queen Elizabeth's reign,
and was enrolled nineteen years later at Christ's College—the Cambridge spawning ground of moderate Puritanism. There he studied
under Laurence Chaderton. He later established his own reputation as
a great teacher with William Ames as his most illustrious pupil. He was
also a friend of Richard Greenham. Like Greenham, Perkins was an accomplished preacher whose "sermons were not so plain but that the
piously-learned did admire them, nor so learned but that the plain did
understand them."[41] He used this gift for more than fifteen years across
the street from Christ's at the church of Great St. Andrews where his
powerful preaching drew large crowds each week. He was interred
there upon his death in 1602, the last year of Elizabeth's reign.

[40]Ibid., 368.

[41]Thomas Fuller quoted in *Dictionary of National Biography*, "William Perkins." On Perkins see also Thomas F. Merrill, ed., *William Perkins* (Nieuw-
koop: B. De Graaf, 1966); Ian Breward, "The Life and Theology of William Perkins" (Ph.D. diss., University of Manchester, 1963); Ian Breward, *The Work of
William Perkins* (Appleford, England: Sutton Courtenay, 1970).

Perkins was an extremely important leader of late-sixteenth-century moderate Puritanism. He was the first Puritan systematic theologian, certainly the first to gain an international reputation. Hence his Sabbath views are of especially great significance.

At least fifty works by Perkins were published in Cambridge between 1590 and 1618. This flood of publications began with the widely-read, immensely popular *Armilla Aurea* which went through three Latin and nine English editions by 1600. The first English translation appeared under the title *A Golden Chaine* in 1591.[42] The Sabbath doctrine found an important place in these early works.

A Golden Chaine is a summary of theology with a strongly decretal, predestinarian emphasis. The subtitle reads "The Description of Theology, containing the order of the causes of Salvation and Damnation, according to God's word." The whole work is divided into two parts, "the first of God, the second of his works."

The first mention of the Sabbath appears early in the second part where Perkins discusses the doctrine of creation—in particular, the creation of mankind. According to Perkins, human subjection to God was to be demonstrated by obedience to two primal commandments: "The one was concerning the two trees: the other, the observation of the Sabbath."[43] In his further development of these two commandments, Perkins pays more attention to the one about the trees than to the one concerning the Sabbath. Nevertheless, his statement introduces the potential for exalting the Sabbath commandment above all others. And, of course, by introducing the Sabbath at this point of mankind's innocence in paradise, Perkins is consistent with those interpretations of the fourth commandment that emphasize its normative, moral, universal roots in the order of creation, and with the later claim that God explicitly addressed the Sabbath commandment to Adam "in his innocency." Although Perkins does not go on to designate Sabbath-breaking as a prominent element in Adam's fall, he does

---

[42]Subsequent references will be from the 1595 edition. *A Golden Chaine* also appears as the first item in Perkins's *Workes*, which were collected and published in three volumes in 1608 and 1609. Perkins may have borrowed the metaphor, "golden chain," from Richard Greenham. See Greenham's *Works*, 63.

[43]Perkins, *A Golden Chaine*, 20.

open the door to the possibility of making the transgression of the Sabbath command one of the most heinous sins.

A more extensive treatment of the Sabbath appears in the lengthy section on the Decalogue, which in turn is included in a section on "the outward means of executing the decree of election."[44] Here Perkins develops his doctrine of the covenant. The Decalogue is "an abridgement of the whole law, and the covenant of works."[45] In his interpretation of each of the ten commandments Perkins shows how the commandment provides indispensable aid in the development of a living, covenant relationship with God.

After discussing various reasons why Christians must still observe the fourth commandment, Perkins addresses the issues of prime importance in Sabbatarianism: the moral versus ceremonial dimensions of the fourth commandment, and the shift from the seventh day to the first. He concedes a ceremonial dimension to the fourth commandment, one aspect of which is the seventh day Sabbath. This seventh day Sabbath has ceased. "The observation of the Sabbath was translated by the Apostles from the seventh day, to the day following," says Perkins. Acts 20:7 and 1 Cor. 16:1–2 make this abundantly clear. The first day of the week, "by reason that our saviour did upon it rise again, is called the Lord's day."[46]

Perkins, nevertheless, affirms the continuing moral relevance of the Sabbath command "in as much as it, as a certain seventh day, preserveth and conserveth the ministry of the word, and the solemn worship of God, especially in the assemblies of the Church. And in this respect we are upon this day, as well enjoined a rest from our vocations, as the Jews were."

Another moral aspect of the Sabbath is "that it freeth servants and cattle from their labours, which on other days do service unto their owners."[47] This latter point may be unique to Perkins. Later Sabbatar-

---

[44]Ibid., 59.

[45]Ibid., 60. Perkins explicitly distinguishes between covenants of grace and of works. In his view the Decalogue is relevant to both, for it continues to guide Christians under grace in covenant living.

[46]Ibid., 102.

[47]Ibid., 102, 103.

ians pay little attention to the moral obligation to release servants and animals from work as a kind of end in itself. Their release from work is primarily, if not exclusively, treated by others as only a means to enhance the full spiritual rest and significance of the day.

The remainder of Perkins's treatment of the Sabbath in *A Golden Chaine* is taken up with a discussion of proper observance of the day. Here, the familiar Sabbath routine is once again elaborated: prayer and preparation, public worship, meditation and conference, and performing works of mercy.[48]

Perkins also discusses the Sabbath at considerable length in the first of his three books on cases of conscience.[49] In these books Perkins demonstrates his skill as a Protestant casuist. Casuistry, before it became pejorative, was simply practical theology, that is, theology set to a pastoral end. In casuistry, or case theology, the author raises the practical questions people were asking, and then attempts to address a word from the Lord to those questions. Late in the sixteenth century many English Protestant leaders were diligently concentrating on this effort. In his preface to the first book, Perkins notes that it is "one special duty of Christ's prophetical office, to give comfort to the consciences of those that are distressed."[50]

Since casuistry was an attempt to deal with problems that were most bothersome to Christians at the time, it is highly significant to notice that one of the cases of conscience on Perkins's agenda was the issue of the Sabbath. This proves that there was a special concern about this issue late in the century, and that not all agreed to the answers to certain questions. It is even more revealing to notice what the most important of these questions was in Perkins's view. For him, "the most principal" of all the questions concerning the Sabbath was the one already raised in the days of the Dedham conference concerning the alteration of the Sabbath and the church's right and freedom to change the day. On this issue, Perkins, like Greenham, takes a forthright Sabbatarian position: "That it is not in the Church's liberty, to alter the

[48]Ibid., 103-105.

[49]William Perkins, *The Whole Treatise of the Cases of Conscience Distinguished into Three Books* (Cambridge: John Legat, 1606).

[50]Ibid., 3.

Sabbath, from the seventh day."[51] He argues that in creation it was God himself who set aside the seventh day and sanctified it "to a holy rest." And in the New Testament it was God in Christ who changed the day. The day was altered, says Perkins, "by Christ himself." That is why it is called "the Lord's day" in Revelation 1:10. Christ "rested on this day from his work of redemption." Just as Christ substituted the Lord's Supper for Passover, so "he substituted the first day of the week in room of the Jew's Sabbath, to be a day set apart to his own worship."[52]

The apostles' example affirms and reinforces this act of Christ. The reference to the weekly collection for the poor on the first day of the week in 1 Corinthians 16:2 suggests that the change to a Sunday Sabbath is an "apostolical and therefore a divine ordinance." Perkins continues, "Yea, that very text doth in some part manifest thus much, that it is an ordinance and institution of Christ. . . . For Paul commandeth nothing but what he had from Christ." He draws upon the practice of the early church for further support of his contention that "this eighth day was without doubt the Lord's day, and so ought to be kept, because it is likely Christ himself kept it holy."[53]

Perkins's argument is unique; it is not found in any other Sabbath treatise. In a bit of remarkable exegesis, he argues that the Sunday Sabbath was foreshadowed in the Old Testament by circumcision on the eighth day. "That which was prefigured, in that it was prefigured was prescribed; but the Lord's day was prefigured in the eighth day, wherein the children of the Jews were circumcised; therefore it was prescribed to be kept the eighth day."[54]

Perkins offers another reason why it is not within the church's authority to change the day of rest and worship. It lies in the principle that "God is Lord of times and seasons, and therefore in all equity, the altering and disposing thereof is in his hands, and belongs to him alone. . . . The Church then, neither may nor can alter the Sabbath day."[55]

---

[51]Ibid., 438.

[52]Ibid., 445.

[53]Ibid., 445, 446.

[54]Ibid., 447.

[55]Ibid., 448.

In the next section in which Perkins deals with objections to the Sunday Sabbath, it is fully apparent that opposition to these Sabbatarian views had arisen. He suggests that opponents have used passages like Colossians 2:16, Galatians 4:10, and Romans 14:5 to prove that the New Testament warns against the distinction of days. Perkins's rejoinder is that these verses deal with ceremonial feast days and not with the Sabbath, which is a perpetual moral law. Furthermore, while it is true that all days are equally fit for the worship of God, "there may be a difference of days in regard of order."[56] In other words, God in his infinite wisdom prescribed a fixed Sabbath, the first day of the week, simply for the good order of the Christian life. In response to the objection that the apostle Paul kept both Saturday and Sunday as days of worship, Perkins argues that in this early stage of the church's history certain concessions were necessary, concessions to the weakness of converted Jews and others who were not yet persuaded of the shift of the day to the first of the week.

In this case of conscience Perkins also deals with questions about proper Sabbath observance. Here he basically repeats the admonitions of Andrewes and Greenham, urging both rest and the dedication of that rest to the holy purpose of worship. Although this rest is not the precise rest of the Old Testament Jews, it involves more than setting aside time for public worship. It requires abandoning ordinary labor as well as "pleasures and recreations."[57] The whole day must be a day of rest and those who insist they need to work in order to maintain themselves and their families must "live by faith, and depend upon God's providence for meat, drink, and clothing."[58] On the other hand, Perkins does concede that there may be works of necessity on the Sabbath and allows some liberty of conscience in making such judgments. He again enumerates the spiritual responsibilities in Sabbath observance: preparation, meditation, public worship, reflection, conference, and works of charity.

Finally, Perkins treats the question of the beginning and extent of the Sabbath day. He takes the position that it begins in the morning

---

[56]Ibid., 450.

[57]Ibid., 456.

[58]Ibid., 457, 458.

and extends to the next morning, not from evening to evening.[59] He argues that this is more in keeping with our view of the other days of the week. Moreover, it was in the morning that Christ arose from the dead. Perkins implicitly holds to a full twenty-four-hour Sabbath.

Perkins's views on the Sabbath are extremely significant. His stature as an early moderate Puritan theologian and the widespread circulation of his writings, as well as his treatment of the Sabbath in cases of conscience demonstrate beyond dispute that the early consensus about the Sabbath had broken down. The central issues of the day of worship and the authority to change that day had become matters that troubled many consciences. In his long argument about the Sunday Sabbath, Perkins reflects the heart of genuine Sabbatarianism.

It is not likely that Sabbatarianism was genetically transmitted, but in Nicholas Bound, we have some evidence that it did run in families. Richard Greenham was his step-father. Bound's sister married John "Decalogue" Dod, the co-author of a very popular treatise which contained a strongly Sabbatarian interpretation of the fourth commandment.

Bound was another one of the Cambridge circle, a fellow of Peterhouse College from 1572 until 1585. In 1585 he was ordained and became pastor of the church in Norton, a small Suffolk village about thirty miles east of Cambridge. In 1611 he moved to the church of St. Andrew the Apostle at Norwich where he died in 1613.

While he was in Norton and involved in a busy parish ministry, Bound wrote two lengthy treatises on the Sabbath, *The Doctrine of the Sabbath* published in 1595, and *Sabbathum Veteris* in 1606.[60] According to the preface, the first of these was based on sermons he had preached early in his tenure at Norton. The preface also testifies to a growing controversy about the Sabbath. "I am not ignorant," writes Bound, "that this argument of the Sabbath is full of controversy, above many other points of divinity, wherein many learned, and godly men dis-

[59]Ibid., 465.

[60]On Bound, see *Dictionary of National Biography*. His two books on the Sabbath will subsequently be identified as *Doctrine* and *Sabbathum*.

sent one from another."[61] Archbishop Whitgift attempted to have
Bound's first book suppressed after its publication in 1595—another
indication that serious disputes about the Sabbath were breaking out
in England.[62] In his preface to the 1606 edition, Bound refers to an earlier aborted effort to prepare an expanded and revised version of
his first book on the Sabbath. He states that he prepared such an edition in 1597 and sent it to the printer only to have it confiscated by the
opposition. He does not identify the culprits, but both Bound and Perkins provide us with incontrovertible evidence that the earlier consensus about the Sabbath in England had broken down. It is also clear in
both Perkins and Bound that the central point of contention was the
issue of alteration, the idea of the Sunday Sabbath.

Taken together, Bound's two books provide us with the classic
statement of English Sabbatarianism. They represent the final stage in
the development of thought and practice regarding the Sabbath. What
others like Andrewes and Greenham and Perkins had said is sharp-
ened and refined in this work. It is also said at much greater length—
286 pages in the first book, and a staggering 459 pages on the fourth
commandment in the 1606 edition.

There is basically little that is new in his books. After reading Andrewes, Greenham, and Perkins, nearly everything in Bound sounds remarkably familiar. In fact, the degree of similarity among all Sabbatarian
treatises is startling. The same arguments, couched in the same familiar phrases, based on the same passages of Scripture, reappear again and
again. Though the authors do not credit one another for ideas, it is obvious that there was a very effective network of communication among
these early Sabbatarians. They had, of course, a common intellectual center in Cambridge. When Andrewes lectured it is likely that Perkins,
Greenham, and Bound heard him. When Perkins published, no doubt
the others read him. Fuller observes that Greenham and Andrewes, both
of Pembroke, were well acquainted and influenced each other's thought.[63]

[61]Nicholas Bound, "To the Godlie and Christian Readers . . .," in *Doctrine* (London, 1595).

[62]See below, 84, 85.

[63]Thomas Fuller, *The Church History of Britain* (London: Tegg and Son, 1837) 3:132.

And in the preface of his first book, Bound acknowledges acquaintance with Greenham's earlier work. Considering these natural alliances, such marked similarities between them are not surprising.

Although the content is familiar, there are some differences between Bound's work and the earlier ones. As we have already noted, in sheer length of treatment Bound far outstrips his predecessors, a clear signal of the arrival of a new phenomenon that might legitimately be called Sabbatarianism. Furthermore, there is evidence in Bound that the high Sabbath positions were hardening. The treatment is sharper, the tone sometimes more dogmatic and contentious than in the earlier treatises. Rather than reviewing the whole line of argument, we will only consider the principal differences between Bound and his predecessors.

In Bound there is a greater stress on the special sanctification of the Sabbath day, on the Sabbath as having almost sacramental stature, and on mankind's absolute dependence upon the Sabbath. The fourth commandment is the most important commandment in the entire Decalogue, he writes, "for in the practice of it, consisteth the practice of all the other, and in the neglect of it is the neglect of all religion."[64] In the following statements we see Bound's essential Sabbatarianism emerging: "God hath bestowed an especial blessing upon this day distinct from the rest, even the blessing of sanctification."[65] Appealing to Frances Junius for support, Bound writes in the second edition, "God did put a special holiness upon this day, above all other; and therefore would have it to be accounted holy of us, and to be spent only in holy uses."[66]

The direct oral communication of the fourth commandment by God in creation is most emphatically stated by Bound when he says that this Sabbath command "was first delivered by lively voice, namely to Adam and Eve in Paradise."[67] Consequently, Bound affirms the enduring, moral character of this commandment, for it "hath so much antiquity, as the seventh day hath being; for so soon as the day was, so soon was it sanctified . . . and as it was in the beginning of the world, so it must

---

[64]Bound, *Doctrine*, 1, 2.

[65]Ibid., 4.

[66]Bound, *Sabbathum*, 292.

[67]Ibid., 11.

continue to the ending of the same."[68] Indeed, for Bound there are *no* ceremonial aspects to the fourth commandment at all. Just as a human being cannot be man and beast at the same time, so a commandment cannot be moral and ceremonial at the same time. In every respect we are as bound to this Sabbath law as ancient Israel was. Even today "we are as precisely to rest as the Jews were."[69] Bound was the first to deny a ceremonial dimension in the fourth commandment. His Sabbatarianism was complete.

Bound comes close to giving the Sabbath sacramental significance and power. Quoting Isaiah 56:4, he argues that through keeping the Sabbath, "the Lord himself would give . . . that which he also promiseth in his covenant, even that knowledge and holiness which he requireth." The Sabbath, for Bound, functioned like a third means of grace, given to us along with the Word and sacraments so that on the Sabbath, "we being so fully and altogether occupied in these means as we should be . . . might through the blessing of God be made partakers of him, who was made of God the father for us wisdom, righteousness, holiness and redemption, and so be saved by him."[70] His statements about the salvific effect of the Sabbath are even stronger and more explicit than those of Richard Greenham. Without the Sabbath we would remain "ignorant, profane and atheists," or at least "dissembling, counterfeit and hypocritical."[71] We need the Sabbath "to bring ourselves back into that estate, from whence we are fallen, and as it were to recover our first footing. . . ."[72] If there were no Sabbath, we should be "most miserable, and should become like unto the rest of the world." Hence, it is a "principal mercy, that the Lord hath reserved it unto us."[73]

Bound is also more emphatic than his predecessors about the alteration issue. He is absolutely committed to a Sunday Sabbath. The

[68]Bound, *Doctrine*, 6.

[69]Bound, *Sabbathum*, 248.

[70]Bound, *Doctrine*, 16, 17.

[71]Ibid., 14.

[72]Ibid., 15.

[73]Ibid., 19.

added emphasis is apparent in the greater length of treatment, but also in his more extreme statement of the matter. He begins the argument by observing that, certainly for the Old Testament Israelites, the Sabbath had to be on the seventh day "and upon none other."[74] In fact, he argues the absoluteness of the seventh day Sabbath so strenuously, that one wonders how he is going to make the shift to the first. It takes fifteen pages of intricate argument but he manages to bring it off. He does so by regarding seventh day and first day as two species of the same genus, the genus Sabbath. The Resurrection of Christ was the turning point, and the apostles' practice of first day worship must be regarded as absolutely authoritative. John's reference to the Lord's day in the first chapter of Revelation proclaims to all "with a loud voice, as it were with the sound of a trumpet" that the day has been changed.[75]

> Now seeing the alteration was made in the Apostles' time, and they did yield unto it by their practise, by whom can we imagine that this should be done, but by them, who had received the spirit, that should lead them into all truth? Than by them (I say) who for their excellent gifts were able to see further into things than all the Church besides; who for their great and apostolical authority could prevail more than any other; who were appointed by Christ, to be the chief builders and planters of the Churches, both in doctrine and discipline?[76]

In keeping with this emphasis, Bound challenges the authority of the church more boldly than either Perkins or Greenham, especially in comments about holy days. The church has no authority to change the Sabbath, but "the holy days may not only be changed, but taken clean away, as coming from men, and the Lord's days as coming from God, not so much as once to be changed."[77] Since the Resurrection was the turning point, it was "not so much the Apostles, as Christ himself" who "brought in this change, and was the author of this day," for it was on this day that Christ Jesus "rested from his work of the new creation." Hence the day must not be changed "unto the end of the world," and "it must not so much as enter into men's thoughts to go about to change

---

[74]Ibid., 30.

[75]Ibid., 40.

[76]Bound, *Sabbathum*, 82, 83.

[77]Ibid., 110.

it."[78] In this the church has no authority, "for it is not a matter of indifference, but a necessary prescription of Christ himself."[79]

Although Bound, like Andrewes, Greenham, and Perkins, ultimately asserts that the Sabbath rest is a means to the end of worship, Bound tends to make the Sabbath rest a kind of end in itself, and to espouse that rest in more stringent, legalistic terms than his predecessors. The Sabbath rest is very special. One can enjoy cessation from labor on other days as well, but "the rest upon this day must be a most careful, exact and precise rest, after another manner, than men for the most part do perform."[80]

For support of this extreme position he relies heavily on Old Testament passages, including those in the Levitical laws. We are with "a double chain" bound to this rest, for we have both social and spiritual need for it. Unlike Adam, we are subject to physical fatigue; like Adam, we need a special time for worship of God. Even the land was supposed to lie idle one year out of seven in Old Testament times. This teaches "of what moment and weight the Sabbath was," that even the "insensible ground should not be free from the subjection of it."[81] In the 1606 edition Bound goes on for nine pages about resting in time of harvest, and discusses for five pages the problem of the Sabbath day's journey.[82]

The threat of legalism looms larger in Bound than in those who preceded him in the development of the Sabbatarian position. In his discussion of what activity is permitted on the Sabbath, he approves of "the ringing of one bell" to call people to service, but not the disordered jangling of many bells.[83] Vices such as drinking, gambling, and dancing are sins on other days of the week, but double-sins on Sunday.[84] We are not only to rest from daily works and pleasures but are

---

[78]Bound, *Doctrine*, 44, 46, 47.

[79]Bound, *Sabbathum*, 67.

[80]Bound, *Doctrine*, 53.

[81]Ibid., 88.

[82]Bound, *Sabbathum*, 134ff., 193ff.

[83]Bound, *Doctrine*, 105.

[84]Ibid., 135.

also prohibited "from speaking and talking of them, seeing his purpose is, not only to restrain the hand and the foot, but the lips and
tongue also."[85] Bound devotes ten graphic pages in the 1606 edition to
the awful punishments that will be meted out upon Sabbath breakers,
cataloging historical instances of people stricken dead, burned, or
maimed for transgressing the Sabbath command.[86] He is also the first
to affirm explicitly a twenty-four-hour Sabbath. He therefore insists that
"we must spend the morning, evening, and whole day, yea some part
of the night, so far as our necessary rest and sleep will permit us in
praising and serving the Lord."[87]

Bound's more stringent Sabbatarianism can be seen, in part, as a
reaction to chaotic worship conditions in the church. He warns hunt-
ers, for example, that proper Sabbath keeping means leaving bows and
arrows and falcons at home. Worshippers should not come to church
"with their bows and arrows in their hands," nor "with their hawks
upon their fists," for these practices could be somewhat distracting. His
response to a falconer's potential objection is based on a Reformed theology of Word and sacrament. He states, "If they themselves would be
ashamed to hold them upon their fists when they should receive the
sacrament, upon what ground do they hold them in the ministry of the
word?"[88]

Apparently, ceaseless traffic in and out of the church also dis-
rupted worship. Bound finds it necessary to insist that the people come
on time and remain until the end of the service.

> For all the people, nay the several households come not together, but
> scattered, and one dropping after another in a confused manner: First
> comes the man, then a quarter of an hour after his wife, and after her,
> I cannot tell how long, especially the maidservants, who must needs be
> as long after her, as the menservants are after him: Whereby it cometh
> to pass that either half the service of God is done before all be met, or
> else if the minister tarry till there be a sufficient congregation, the first

[85]Ibid., 137.

[86]Bound, *Sabbathum*, 252-62.

[87]Ibid., 374.

[88]Bound, *Doctrine*, 132, 133.

comers may be weary, and sometimes cold with tarrying, before the
other shall be warm in their seats.[89]

The people, selective about which part of the worship service they
wished to attend, apparently came and went at will. "Some under
pretence of coming to the sermon, tarry at home a great part of the service, and so neither are they at the confession of sin with God's people, nor are made partakers of the prayers of the Church for the
forgiveness of their sins, neither do ever hear much of the Scripture
read: other under colour of being at all these depart away before the
blessing is pronounced upon them . . . or else tarry not the minister-
ing of the sacrament, as though it were a thing impertinent unto
them."[90] So to enhance the good order of the service, Bound urges that
the people "be present at the whole action."

Additional disorder surrounded the mechanics of alms-giving during divine worship. In the midst of the service in many churches, Bound
claims that "you shall see men go up and down asking, receiving,
changing, and bestowing of money, wherein many times you shall have
them so disagree, that they are louder than the minister; and the rest
stand looking, and listening unto them, leaving the worship of God
(as though it did not concern them) and thus all is confused." Consequently, he urges that alms be gathered at "some other time of the day
. . . to bestow at the end of the service upon the needy."[91]

In the 1606 edition Bound issues one more complaint about disorder.
He objects, not unreasonably, to the presence of dogs in church. He complains, "they are as troublesome to the ears with their mouths . . . and
more offensive to the eye . . . And if one man may be permitted to bring
his dog to the Church, why might not another, and why might not all?
And then what a thing were this to have in a place an hundred or two
hundred dogs together . . . and that in time of divine service."[92]

Such worship conditions no doubt played a role in the development of a stricter and more orderly Sabbath observance. The disci-

---

[89]Ibid., 268.

[90]Ibid., 175.

[91]Ibid., 193.

[92]Bound, *Sabbathum*, 264-65.

plined Sabbath promoted and supported with appeals to divine commandment must have been an attractive option to many who were disturbed by the abuse of the Sabbath and by disorder in the service of public worship.

Bound's prescriptions for Sabbath observance include nothing that is really new, but again his treatment is much more extensive and detailed than that of his predecessors. Preparation for worship includes self-examination, prayer, and reading of the Scriptures. Following the services, reflection and meditation is prescribed. For seven pages Bound extols the practice of meditation. The godliest men, he says, are not necessarily "the greatest hearers and readers of the Word," but are rather "the greatest musers and meditators thereon."[93]

Family discussion of the sermon and Psalm singing are other important Sabbath activities. The social emphasis is also present, for the Lord's day is "the day of showing mercy."[94] The worship of God is ordained to one end: that we be better equipped to show love to others. Bound states that we must, therefore, feed the hungry, clothe the naked, lodge the harborless, and visit the sick and prisoners, especially on the Sabbath.

Bound concludes his Sabbath expositions with a challenge to those in authority both in the commonwealth and in individual families to enact good laws compelling all people to sanctify the Sabbath. Sabbath desecration, after all, is the underlying cause for all of society's evils including rebellious children, disobedient servants, and unfaithful wives.[95]

Sabbatarianism reached its zenith in England with Nicholas Bound. Andrewes, Greenham, and Perkins were Sabbath heavyweights in their contributions to the development of the position, but in Bound it blooms to full flower. Bound's statement is classic in the length and detail of his treatment, in the more contentious tone of his writing, and in his more complete development of the three dimensions of Sabba-

[93]Bound, *Doctrine*, 208.

[94]Ibid., 247.

[95]Ibid., 271.

tarianism—the moral, creational character of the fourth commandment, the stringent rules of observance and, most important, the emphatic commitment to Sunday absolutism. Indeed, no one developed the position more fully after Bound completed his prodigious works. Scores of treatises on the Sabbath appeared in the next fifty years, but they simply restated his views. And in the 1640s, Bound's views would become enshrined in the Westminster Confession with its appeal to the "law of nature" in support of the Sabbath, its reference to the fourth commandment as a "moral, and perpetual commandment binding all men in all ages," and with its insistence that the Sabbath day "from the beginning of the world to the resurrection of Christ, was the last day of the week; and, from the resurrection of Christ, was changed into the first day of the week . . . and is to be continued to the end of the world, as the Christian sabbath."[96] One can imagine the Westminster divines working on these articles with an open volume of Bound's *Sabbathum Veteris* before them.

Meanwhile, Bound's work aroused an angry anti-Sabbatarianism. As we have seen, there was discussion and dispute about the Sabbath beginning in the 1580s, but prior to the end of the century there is no evidence of any organized opposition. The Cambridge circle had built upon a long tradition of high Sabbath views in England. But when Greenham, Perkins, and Bound took the position of Sunday absolutism, thereby challenging the church's authority, they took one step too far. At the turn of the century the Establishment reacted and anti-Sabbatarianism was born.

---

[96]*The Westminister Confession of Faith*, chap. 21, sec. 7.

4

THE
RISE OF ANTI-SABBATARIANISM

SINCE THE EARLY DAYS of the Reformation, at least as early as the reign of Edward VI, there was a strong Sabbath motif in the life and thought of the Church of England. The emphasis on faithful Sabbath observance gained momentum as the sixteenth century progressed, but there is evidence that in the 1580s the widespread doctrinal consensus about the Sabbath was beginning to break down. By the end of the century traditional Sabbath views had evolved into full-blown Sabbatarianism, an interpretation of the fourth commandment that included not only the familiar emphases on the moral character of that commandment and on the need for its strict observance, but also the articulation of the view that the first day of the week is the New Testament Sabbath by divine design. This view can be traced way back to John Hooper in the 1540s, but the doctrine of Sunday absolutism was resurrected later in the century. It was refined and elaborated in much greater detail, especially by Nicholas Bound. It was this doctrine that touched off the anti-Sabbatarian reaction.

Earlier decades had been marked by the relative absence of official controversy about the Sabbath. There is no evidence that the strong Sabbath-keeping sermons of Northbrooke, Field, Stubbes, and others provoked hostile reactions, official or otherwise. The public lectures of Lancelot Andrewes attracted large audiences in Cambridge around 1580, but they did not create controversy. There is likewise no evidence of attacks on Greenham and Perkins for their development of strong Sabbath positions.

There were only two early indicators of trouble on the horizon: the controversy at Dedham in the 1580s, and a small problem at Cambridge in that same decade. John Strype reports that a man named John Smith preached a sermon in Cambridge in 1585 in which some comments about Sabbath breaking "gave occasion of offense."[1] People especially disagreed with his insistence that the Sabbath be strictly observed for a twenty-four-hour period, but the matter was settled at the local level without the ripple effect of widespread controversy.

Changes began to occur in the waning days of the century. The church establishment apparently decided to get tough with Nicholas Bound; something in his 1595 treatise touched an exposed nerve. In 1599 Archbishop Whitgift "by his letters and officers at synods and visitations" ordered that Bound's book be "called in and forbidden any more to be printed and made common."[2] Shortly thereafter, Sir John Popham, Lord Chief Justice of England, issued a similar order against the book. According to Bound, anti-Sabbatarian activity began as early as 1597. In his preface to the 1606 edition he mentions that he had prepared a second edition of his earlier treatise, had sent it off to the printer, but that it had been confiscated "and so hitherto hath been suppressed."[3]

We have no direct evidence from Whitgift's own hand as to why he decided to suppress Bound's book. Kenneth Parker suggests that Whitgift, for certain political reasons, was more incensed about the dedication of Bound's book to Robert Devereux, Earl of Essex, than he was about the content of the Sabbatarian position.[4] Though this is an interesting hypothesis, it lacks concrete evidence. On the other hand, it is beyond dispute that disagreements about the Sabbath were beginning to arise in the church toward the end of the century. It is also ev-

---

[1] John Strype, *Annals of the Reformation* vol.3 (Oxford: Clarendon Press, 1824) 494, 497.

[2] Thomas Rogers, *The Catholic Doctrine of the Church of England* (Cambridge: Parker Society, 1854) 20.

[3] *Sabbathum Veteris*, A 3.

[4] *The English Sabbath*, (Cambridge: at the University Press, 1988) 95-97.

ident that Nicholas Bound brought Sabbatarian doctrine to its apogee with his emphatic claims for a first-day, Sunday Sabbath established by divine right. Against the background of Whitgift's long struggles with Thomas Cartwright and the presbyterian movement, with Puritan prophesyings and the classis movement, and with non-conformity, it is easy to understand why he would be extremely sensitive to any newly developing challenges to the authority of church and state.

In fact, it is helpful in our understanding of Whitgift's reaction to Bound to observe that the issue of the church's authority in relation to the appointment of a day of worship had been debated earlier in the Whitgift-Cartwright debates over the *Admonition to Parliament* back in the 1570s. The *Admonition* was Cartwright's plea for the introduction of a presbyterian system of government in the Church of England.[5] It stated that all of worship should be determined by the will of God revealed in the Scriptures. Whitgift's answer included this comment: "The Scripture hath not appointed what day in the week shoud be most meet for the sabbath-day, whether Saturday, which is the Jew's sabbath, or the day now observed, which was appointed by the church."[6] In his reply, Cartwright did not take a strong position on the matter, but doubted that the church now had the right to alter the day. In his counter response, Whitgift skirts the issue of alteration, but later in the debate he argues that to celebrate the Lord's day on Sunday is not a matter of divine commandment but of churchly custom, which is to say, "it is no matter of religion, but of civility and order."[7] This early exchange between Whitgift and Cartwright throws some light on Whitgift's reaction when Bound raised the same issues in 1595, and also lends some credence to the establishment's fear that Sabbatarianism and Presbyterianism were at least subtly linked. These fears, at any rate, were not imaginary. And even if in reality Sabbatarianism was not the offspring of Presbyterianism, anti-Sabbatarianism was certainly a direct descendent of anti-Presbyterianism. The first anti-Sabbatarian ar-

---

[5]Donald J. McGinn, *The Admonition Controversy* (New Brunswick: Rutgers University Press, 1949); Peter Lake, *Anglicans and Puritans?* (London: Unwin Hyman, 1988).

[6]John Whitgift, *Works* vol.1 (Cambridge: Parker Society, 1851) 1:200.

[7]Ibid., 1:200-202; 3:368.

guments are virtually identical to anti-Presbyterian arguments. Anti-Sabbatarianism had its origin in the earlier Whitgift-Cartwright debates.

In the last month of the century Thomas Rogers entered the fray. On 10 December 1599 he preached a stinging sermon against Bound's Sabbatarian position in Bury St. Edmunds, just seven miles from Bound's church in Norton. Rogers was a chaplain of Richard Bancroft who had been active in the establishment's anti-Presbyterian campaign. Rogers had been trained at Oxford (Christ's College), and was installed as rector of Horringer in Suffolk in 1581. There he found himself in the midst of a number of "godly preachers" with Puritan sympathies, from whom he secluded himself and by whom he was deliberately excluded in part because of his strong stand against Presbyterianism. So there was no love lost between Rogers and his Suffolk neighbor, Nicholas Bound, one of the circle of godly preachers. According to Rogers's own testimony, he was the founder of anti-Sabbatarianism. He claimed, in *The Catholic Doctrine* published in 1607, that he had alerted authorities like Whitgift and Popham to the insidious heresy of Sabbatarianism and of links between Sabbatarianism and Presbyterianism.[8] His December 1599 sermon is very significant in the history of Sabbatarianism, for it may well be the occasion when the movement received its name.

In any case, the notes taken by someone present at the sermon contain our earliest documented reference to Sabbatarians. As we have seen, these notes reveal clearly the central issue for Rogers. He does not debate the moral character of the fourth commandment or question the importance of a weekly day of rest and worship. The target of his attack is the relatively new claim made by Bound concerning the day, namely, that a New Testament Lord's day or Sabbath day has been instituted by divine authority. The notes in their entirety follow:

> That we Christians of the Church of England are bound to keep the Sabbath day is antichristian and unsound; 2. that the Sabbath is of the nature of tithes, of new moons, and Jewish feasts; 3. not possible to be proved that the Jews before the coming out of Egypt kept a Sabbath; 4. no certain day commanded for Christians in the Word of God more than other; 5. the Lord's day is not enjoined by God's commandment but by

---

[8]Rogers, *Catholic Doctrine*, 20.

an human civil and ecclesiastical constitution. 6. He thinketh that the days commonly called the Lord's days, Sabbath days, or Sundays may be called the Queen's days and that he would so call them, and so did oftentimes in his sermon. 7. Those which hold that opinion against which he himself preached he called Sabbatarians and dominicans. 8. Since weekly days have gone up her majesty's days have gone down . . . [from] papistry and Brownism sects of sabbatarians and dominicans have sprung. 9. The Queen bindeth us by her days but she bindeth us not, our dominicans do bind and fetter us. 10. The observation of the Queen's day do [sic] not make or hinder salvation but if we keep not the Lord's day we shall perish say the Sabbatarians. 11. He finally declared that if this might deny God he would not further proceed in this question, otherwise this his speech was but an entrance. Master Rogers' sermon preached at Bury the 10. Dec. 1599.[9]

A few years later Rogers tightened the link between Presbyterianism and Sabbatarianism in his 1607 publication of *The Catholic Doctrine.* Actually, this written attack on Sabbatarianism was slow in coming. Thomas Fuller mentions with regard to Bound that for several years after the attempted suppression by Whitgift, "not so much as a feather of a quill in print did wag against him."[10] But when the charge was mounted, it came with intensity. Thomas Rogers was now the archbishop's chaplain, for Richard Bancroft had succeeded Whitgift in 1604. *The Catholic Doctrine* was a commentary on the "Thirty-nine Articles," the basic credal statement of the Church of England. In this work Rogers valiantly defends England's orthodoxy from a variety of contemporary errors and heresies. One of these heresies is Sabbatarianism, which he attacks with venom. His fusillade confirms that the Establishment was convinced of a clear and direct connection between Sabbatarianism and the aborted presbyterian effort. Apparently, the authorities at Lambeth believed that Sabbatarianism was simply Presbyterianism in new dress, making it fatally dangerous to church and commonwealth, and, therefore, a movement to be suppressed at all costs.

In his preface Rogers rejoices that the presbyterian movement had finally been "exploded out of this Christian Kingdom" by the joint ef-

---

[9]Townshend Papers, vol.1, ms. 38492, fol. 104, The British Library, London.

[10]Thomas Fuller, *The Church History of Britain* (London: Tegg and Son, 1837) 160.

forts of the queen and archbishop in 1588. The blows inflicted on that diabolical heresy had mortally wounded the presbyterian cause, for Her Majesty and Whitgift had "so battered the new discipline as hitherto they could never, nor hereafter shall ever fortify and repair the decays thereof."[11] (Mercifully Rogers did not have to live to see the developments of the 1640s.)

But though the evil cause was laid to rest, its promoters lived on and they were not lacking for new stratagems to disrupt church and kingdom. His view of the continuity between Presbyterianism and Sabbatarianism is worth quoting in full. It reads,

> Notwithstanding, what the brethen wanted in strength and learning, they had in wiliness; and, though they lost much one way in the general and main point of their discipline, yet recovered they not a little advantage another way, by an odd and a new device of theirs, in a special article of their classical instructions. For while these worthies of our Church were employing their engines and forces, partly in defending the present government ecclesiastical, partly in assaulting the presbytery and new discipline, even at that very instant the brethen (knowing themselves too weak either to overthrow our holds, and that which we hold, or to maintain their own) they abandoned quite the bulwarks which they had raised, and gave out were impregnable; suffering us to beat them down, without any, or very small resistance: and yet not careless of their affairs, left not the wars for all that, but from an odd corner, and after a new fashion, which we little thought of (such was their cunning), set upon us afresh again by dispersing in printed books (which for ten years' space before they had been in hammering among themselves to make them complete) their Sabbath speculations, and presbyterian (that is, more than either kingly or popely) directions for the observation of the Lord's day.[12]

Rogers uncovers a sore spot when he complains that the Sabbatarians "at one blow beat down all time and days," denying the church's authority to set aside any day but the Lord's day. "They build not presbyteries expressedly (though under hand, if it be well marked, they do erect them in their exercises of the Sabbath:) but they set up a new idol, their Saint Sabbath . . . in the midst, and minds of God's people." The Sabbatarian attack on all holy days other than the Sabbath,

[11]Rogers, *Catholic Doctrine*, 17.

[12]Ibid., 17, 18.

Rogers believes, would lead to great licentiousness in the land, for the result would be "gross contempt of the necessary and laudable orders of our Churches."[13]

Rogers's summary of Sabbatarian doctrine, while inadequate and incomplete, reveals his central concern: the issue of the day. He suggests in the second point of his summary that the Sabbatarians are assuming authority that is not theirs: "Their doctrine summarily may be reduced unto these two heads, whereof the one is, that the Lord's day, even as the old Sabbath was of the Jews, must necessarily be kept, and solemnized of all and every Christian, under the pain of eternal condemnation both of body and soul. The other, that under the same penalty it must be kept from the highest to the lowest, both of King and people, in sort and manner as these brethren among themselves have devised, decreed, and prescribed."[14]

Rogers's description of Sabbatarian doctrine may be inadequate, but his primary concern as a spokesman for the Establishment is unmistakeable. He is concerned about the maintenance of the church's authority in such matters as providing for a day of worship and prescription of holy days. For if the church has no authority in these areas, where would the line be drawn? Sedition and anarchy would be inevitable. Because Rogers sees the issue in the one-dimensional perspective of ecclesiastical authority, he regards Sabbatarianism as virtually equivalent to Presbyterianism. He says after reading Bound's book, obviously with Thomas Cartwright in mind, "I presently smelt . . . whose disciples all those preachers are."[15] Rogers does not reveal the identity of "all those preachers," but the phrase apparently includes Sabbatarians.

Rogers makes several disparaging references to another earlier presbyterian concern: Bound's strong emphasis on a preaching ministry. "Yet think we not (which our Sabbatarians let not to publish) that every minister necessarily, and under pain of damnation, is to preach at least once every Sunday; and, unless a minister preach every Sun-

---

[13]Ibid., 18. Cf. 183, 315, 322.

[14]Ibid., 19.

[15]Ibid., 20.

day, he doth not hallow the Sabbath day."[16] He also claims that "their doctrine is to the common people, that, unless they leave their un-preaching ministers every Sabbath day, and go to some place where the word is preached they do profane the Sabbath, and subject them-selves unto the curse of God."[17] This charge, even if overstated, re-flects an important difference between the Establishment and Sabba-tarians on the importance of hearing the preached Word.

The extravagance of Rogers's attack is exemplified in his charge that "this Sabbath doctrine of the brethren agreeth neither with the doc-trine of our Church, nor with the laws and orders of this kingdom; dis-turbeth the peace both of the Commonweal, and Church; and tendeth unto schism in the one, and sedition in the other. . . ."[18] Such allega-tions, to be repeated many times, led to the polarization of the Church of England into Anglican and Puritan camps in the seventeenth cen-tury. When Rogers's view of the situation became the official party view, it became more and more difficult for Sabbatarians to remain loyal Anglicans. Anglicanism and Puritanism were tragically driven apart in the seventeenth century, not only by intemperate Puritans but also by intemperate Establishment figures who could no longer tolerate Puri-tan Sabbatarians in the church. The Establishment refused to believe that Sabbatarians such as Nicholas Bound were capable of basic loyalty to church and state and only wanted the parish churches to use the day of worship more effectively to bring about a higher level of Christian knowledge and virtue in the lives of the people for the benefit of church and commonwealth. If the church's hierarchy could have accepted that, the course of seventeenth-century English history might have been profoundly altered. They adopted an approach that polarized rather than healed, and the results were disastrous. The parties were driven to irreconcilable extremes.

———————————

This is not to say that there were no fundamental differences be-tween Sabbatarians and their opponents. David Little has argued that

[16]Ibid., 233.

[17]Ibid., 271.

[18]Ibid., 20.

the basic difference between Puritans and Anglicans was legal, a clash between two "patterns of order" and that "the heart of Puritan thought rested in its advocacy of a new basis for obedience and a new form of authority."[19] This analysis is helpful in interpreting the clash between Sabbatarians and anti-Sabbatarians. The authority issue had loomed large since the very beginning of English Protestantism. The Reformation in England, more than anywhere else, was a struggle over authority from the moment Henry VIII challenged the power of the Vatican. Questions of authority involving Scripture, church administration, and the state were at the center of the debates over matters of worship since the days of Edward VI. As its name suggests, the presbyterian movement was essentially an attempt to alter the authority structure of the church. It is not surprising, therefore, that the real issue dividing the Sabbatarians and anti-Sabbatarians was the issue of authority in relation to the day of worship.

This issue came into clearest focus through the discussion of the interrelated topics of alteration and holy days. "Alteration" is the label that was commonly used for the change of the day of worship from the Old Testament seventh day to the New Testament first day. The Sabbatarians insisted that this alteration came about by divine authority while the anti-Sabbatarians insisted that the change was solely a matter of church tradition. Every anti-Sabbatarian treatise focused on this issue. In fact, beginning with Thomas Rogers, anti-Sabbatarians tended to read all the teachings of the Sabbatarians in terms of the authority issue. In his preface to John Prideaux's Sabbath treatise, Peter Heylyn summarizes Sabbatarian thought under seven heads, all of which center in the authority issue. Presbyterianism and Sabbatarianism are inseparably linked in Heylyn's mind. "But in the year 1595, some of that faction which before had labored with small profit, to overthrow the hierarchy and government of the Church of England; now set themselves on work to ruinate all the orders of it: to beat down at one blow all days and times, which by the wisdom and authority of the Church, has been appointed for God's service, and in the stead thereof to erect a Sabbath, of their own devising."[20]

---

[19]David Little, *Religion, Order and Law* (Oxford: Basil Blackwell, 1970) 31. Cf. 15ff., 27-28, 168.

[20]Peter Heylyn, *History of the Sabbath*, vol. 2, 250.

Why was this matter of alteration and the claim for divine right for a Sunday Sabbath so important to the anti-Sabbatarians? In practice these issues appear to be incidental and inconsequential. No one was making a serious move toward actually having the church alter the day of worship to, say, Tuesday or Thursday. Yet the anti-Sabbatarians were convinced that a fundamental principle was at stake: the freedom of the church to establish ceremonies, holy days, and a host of other worship practices as the church saw fit. This principle was clearly reflected in Richard Hooker, who held a high Sabbath view and yet was exceedingly interested in protecting the authority of the church. To curtail the church's authority to appoint days of worship and other holy days "shaketh universally the fabric of government, tendeth to anarchy and mere confusion, dissolveth families, dissipateth colleges, corporations, armies, overthroweth kingdoms, churches, and whatsoever is now through the providence of God by authority and power upheld."[21]

The dispute about holy days, traditionally instituted and authorized by the church, was a closely related issue and eventually became a part of the Sabbath debate. Cartwright and Whitgift had also argued this matter at great length in their debates over the *Admonition to Parliament*. When it was mentioned again by Sabbatarians late in the century, Whitgift quickly became attuned to the matter. This may also explain his decision to take action against the Sabbatarianism of Nicholas Bound.

Cartwright, however, had raised the issue of holy days in the context of God's permission of six days of labor rather than in the context of the command for a day of rest. He opposed holy days on the ground that they interfere with a divinely established human right: the freedom to perform the works of our callings for a full six days a week. "Seeing that therefore the Lord hath left it to all men at liberty that they might labour, if they think good, six days," he argued, "I say, the church, nor no man, can take this liberty from them, and drive them

---

[21]Richard Hooker, *Of the Laws of Ecclesiastical Polity, the Fifth Book*, ed., Ronald Bayne (London: Macmillan, 1902), 422. With regard to the anti-Sabbatarians and the institution of the Sabbath day, Samuel Gardiner says, "Their reverence for church authority led them to shrink from tracing its institution higher than to the earliest Christian times." *History of England* vol. 3, (London: Longmans, Green, & Co., 1883) 3:250.

to a necessary rest of the body."[22] He objected to the proliferation of holy days also for social reasons. They are "a thing which breedeth idleness and consequently poverty, besides other disorders and vices which always go in company with idleness."[23]

The holy day problem arose again in connection with the authority on which the Sabbath day rests. The Sabbatarian insistence on divine right for that day naturally led to the questioning of the status of any church-appointed days of worship whatsoever. Regarding the observance of a Christmas day, for example, William Perkins wrote, "The feast of the nativity of our saviour is only a custom and tradition of the church and yet men are commonly more careful to keep it than the Lord's day, the keeping whereof stands by the moral law."[24] Nicholas Bound tactlessly linked the observance of holy days with "papistry," although he did not unleash a full-scale attack on them as Thomas Rogers suggests.[25] John Dod similarly complained that people observed the holy days more faithfully than the Sabbath. "And most of them have no care of the sabbath, but have more regard of their idol holy-days, which the Pope hath appointed, than of the Sabbath day, which God hath commanded."[26] Thomas Fuller accurately perceived that, again, the church's authority lay at the root of this problem. He observed that some believed that the Sabbath doctrine put an "unequal lustre on the Sunday on set purpose to eclipse all other holy-days, to the derogation of the authority of the church."[27] Richard Hooker was convinced that nothing less than the good order of the entire commonwealth was at stake if the church's authority to designate holy days were curtailed, for the result would be anarchy.

---

[22]Whitgift, *Works* (Cambridge: Parker Society, 1851) vol. 2, 569.

[23]Ibid., 2:587.

[24]*The Work of William Perkins*, ed., I. Breward (Appleford: Sutton Courtenay, 1970) 555.

[25]Rogers, *Catholic Doctrine*, 32.

[26]John Dod, *A Plaine and Familiar Exposition of the Ten Commandements* (London, 1632) 10.

[27]Fuller, *Church History*, 3:160.

Those things which the law of God leaveth arbitrary and at liberty are all subject unto positive laws of men, which laws for the common benefit bridge particular men's liberty in such things as far as the rule of equity will suffer. This we must maintain, or else overturn the world and make every man his own commander. Seeing then that labour and rest upon any one day of the six throughout the year are granted free by the law of God, how exempt we them from the force and power of ecclesiastical law, except we deprive the world of power to make any ordinance of law at all?[28]

Peter Heylyn charged that the Sabbatarians' attack on holy days was intended from the first moment "these Sabbath doctrines peeped into light."[29]

In fully developed Sabbatarianism the authority issue became central in the case for the first-day Sabbath, and since the issues of alteration and holy days were already present in the Whitgift-Cartwright debates, it is not surprising that Rogers and all of his anti-Sabbatarian successors suspected a Presbyterian-Sabbatarian collusion. As a matter of fact, there *was* a connection as suggested in the analysis of the Dedham debates. In the spate of anti-Sabbatarian literature in the 1620s and 1630s Sabbatarianism and Presbyterianism continued to be regarded as twin heresies in the Church of England. They were both regarded as attempts to overthrow the established order. Bishop White's dedicatory to Archbishop Laud in the preface of his book against Theophilus Brabourne's extreme Sabbatarianism explicitly makes the connection with Cartwright. He hopes that his book "may be a means to settle the Sabbatarian Controversy, which ever since Thomas Cartwright's unlucky days, hath disquieted both Church and State." The Sabbatarians and Presbyterians together are all "schismatical spirits."[30]

Presbyterians and Sabbatarians are also lumped together by Bishop White in his charge of "neglect and contempt" of the *Book of Common Prayer*. This sacrilege, White writes, "had his beginning from the Presbyterians," and "now lately, since I have been reading many English pamphlets and tractates of the Sabbath, I can hardly find any treatise wherein the use of the Common Service by the ministers, and the due

---

[28]Hooker, *Ecclesiastical Polity*, 423.

[29]Heylyn, *History of the Sabbath*, 2:255.

[30]F. White, *A Treatise of the Sabbath-Day* (London, 1635) fol. A4.

frequenting thereof by the people, is once named among the duties or offices of sanctifying the Lord's day."[31] Instead, "an indigested form and conception of extemporal prayer is used."[32]

In another important anti-Sabbatarian treatise written in 1636, John Pocklington points to similarities between Presbyterians and Sabbatarians in their concern for preaching as well as in the "attack" on the prayer book. He sees revolutionary motives inspiring both groups, for both Presbyterians and Sabbatarians are involved in attacks on the present order and law of the land in church and state. He regards such revolution as the true agenda of both the early and current Sabbatarians, because, as he states, "You see then what the plot was that bred, and still keeps the name of Sabbath on foot."[33] He laments that the *Prayer Book* is another target of the Sabbatarians. They "uphold the name of Sabbath, that stalking behind it they may shoot against the service appointed for the Lord's day."[34] Hence the Sabbatarians were "a disease, a fretting canker, a dangerous faction in the Church."[35]

Pocklington sets these charges in the context of the Sabbatarians' "casting out of lawful sports." In 1618 King James added the Sabbath recreation issue to those to be hotly debated in the 1620s. The question of lawful sports on the Sabbath of course was not a new one. The *King's Book* of 1543, and the *Homily of the Place and Time of Prayer* in 1560 both issued warnings against allowing sport and recreation to interfere with proper Sabbath keeping. William Whitaker has shown that there was legislation against tennis and football on Sunday as early as the days of Richard II.[36] And both Whitaker and Kenneth Parker demonstrate convincingly that during Elizabeth's reign there was a large body of public opinion that assumed that proper Sabbath keeping involved the curbing of sport and recreation on the day of worship. Christopher Hill

---

[31]Ibid., fol. A3.

[32]Ibid., fol. ** 2.

[33]John Pocklington, *Sunday No Sabbath* (London: Robert Young, 1636) 8.

[34]Ibid., 20.

[35]Ibid., 40.

[36]William B. Whitaker, *Sunday in Tudor and Stuart Times* (London: Houghton, 1933) 12, 13.

also argues that opposition to Sunday sport was "not merely a fad of Puritan ministers," but had broad public support.[37]

Perhaps the king was either ignorant of or indifferent to public opinion. In any case, he issued his *Book of Sports* on 24 May 1618,[38] prompted by a stop in Lancashire on his way home from a visit to Scotland. There he discovered some particularly stringent local laws against recreation on the Sabbath. He proceeded to "rebuke some Puritans and precise people, and took order that the like unlawful carriage should not be used by any of them hereafter, in the prohibiting and unlawful punishing of our good people for using their lawful recreations, and honest exercises upon Sundays and other holy days, after the afternoon sermon or service."[39] He discovered later that both "Papists and Puritans" had "maliciously traduced and calumniated" his orders. He decided to issue the *Book of Sports* to clarify his position.

In his book the king notes the presence of a large number of "popish recusants" in Lancashire, and in this connection states one of his motives for his ruling on Sabbath recreation: it is an unnecessary stumbling block to the conversion of Catholics to Protestantism, for "their priests will take occasion hereby to vex, persuading them that no honest mirth or recreation is lawful or tolerable in our religion, which cannot but breed a great discontentment in our peoples' hearts, especially of such as are peradventure upon the point of turning." The other motive was the king's concern for physical fitness. Prohibiting sport and recreation on Sunday "barreth the common and meaner sort of people from using such exercises as may make their bodies more able for war, when we or our successors shall have occasion to use them."[40] After all, "when shall the common people have leave to exercise, if not upon the Sundays and holy days, seeing they must apply their labour, and win their living in all working days?" Therefore he decrees "no lawful recreation shall be barred to our good people, which shall not tend to

---

[37]*Society and Puritanism in Pre-Revolutionary England* (New York: Schocken, 1964) 202-205.

[38]*The Kings Majesties Declaration to His Subjects, Concerning lawfull Sports to be used* (London: Norton and Bill, 1618).

[39]Ibid., 2.

[40]Ibid., 4.

the breach of our aforesaid Laws, and canons of Our Church."[41] In a rather inflammatory statement he declares that "Puritans and Precisians" must either "conform themselves" or "leave the country."[42]

The reaction of the Sabbatarians was a stunned silence. Few Sabbatarian treatises appeared in the decade following the publication of the *Book of Sports,* but for that matter there was a marked absence of gloating in anti-Sabbatarian literature as well. One wonders if many really thought it was a good and wise decree. Even the archbishop, George Abbot, is said to have been displeased with the king's proclamation and decided to "refuse compliance" with the order to read it from pulpits.[43] William Prynne, commenting on Archbishop Laud's later support of the king, declared, "What could Beelzebub, had he been the Archbishop, have done more than in publishing the book against Sunday."[44] Thomas Fuller thought it a disaster, stating that many moderates in the seventeenth century regarded the king's action "a principal cause of the civil war."[45] Later in 1633 when Charles reissued the *Book of Sports* and Laud gave it the full support of his office, it most certainly had a polarizing effect, forcing people to choose sides, and widening the breach between Anglicans and Puritans.

David Little regards "a deep-seated conflict over the problem of order"[46] as the fundamental issue dividing Puritans and Anglicans. We have demonstrated that at least from the anti-Sabbatarian perspective, the problem of order and authority was indeed fundamental. It should be said, however, that it is not clearly evident from Sabbatarian literature that Sabbatarians were consciously and deliberately attacking the traditional order. In the Sabbatarian treatises, particularly the early ones written for the most part by moderate Puritans, there is every indication of willingness to accept the established order and framework of

---

[41]Ibid., 5.

[42]Ibid., 6.

[43]Gardiner, *History of England,* 3:252.

[44]Quoted in C. Hill, *Society and Puritanism,* 193.

[45]Fuller, *Church History,* 3:378-79.

[46]*Religion, Order, and Law,* 168. Cf. Patrick Collinson, *English Puritanism* (London: The Historical Association, 1983) 15, 16.

church and state. One suspects that Whitgift, Rogers, Bancroft, Pocklington, White, Heylyn, and, of course, Laud, overreacted to a relatively innocent Sabbatarianism that sought not to overthrow the
traditional structures of church and state, but whose design was simply that of all moderate Puritans: spiritual renewal in the lives of the
people.

Sabbatarianism was not a radical movement with a hidden revolutionary agenda spawned by frustrated Presbyterians but was an
honest, well-meaning effort on the part of moderates basically loyal to
church and state to bring about spiritual and moral improvement in the
lives of the people and hence to the nation. This effort was to be un-
dertaken within the framework of traditional government and without
a particularly "revolutionary" impulse.

Anti-Sabbatarianism, on the other hand, was an unnecessarily harsh
response to this moderate movement. It was a reactionary move to the
right, a deeper and more conservative retrenchment into conformity
rather than reformation. In anti-Sabbatarianism there are traces of a
theological position that departed from the Reformation norm of
Scripture alone as its authority, and deliberately and self-consciously
adopted tradition and the law of reason as the determinatives for action. Typically, Puritanism is charged with introducing a "new basis
for obedience and a new form of authority" into the English church.[47]
But if Luther and Calvin provide the norm, it was the Anglicanism of
Whitgift and Hooker, and especially of Laud, that adopted a new form
of authority. This is not to suggest an equation between these early anti-
Sabbatarians and Nicholas Tyacke's anti-Calvinists.[48] The parallels between these movements—which both apparently arose within the
Church of England during the same decades—seem striking, but the
events and issues are much too complex to permit a simplified reading. It is impossible to draw lines of internal relationship between Sabbatarianism and Calvinistic predestinarian theology, or between anti-
Sabbatarianism and Arminianism. It would be outrageous to suggest
that early anti-Sabbatarians like Rogers and Whitgift were anti-Calvin-
istic Arminians. It is more likely that there existed a broader complex

[47]*Religion, Order, and Law*, 31.

[48]Nicholas Tyacke, *Anti-Calvinists: The Rise of English Arminianism* (Oxford:
Clarendon Press, 1987).

of ecclesiastical and theological circumstances that helped to give birth to both movements. We shall consider these in later chapters. It is also likely that for political reasons, a realignment of parties and convergence of movements took place later on, in the 1620s and 1630s, when it becomes more plausible to align Arminians with anti-Sabbatarians and Sabbatarians with Calvinistic Puritans.

Although Sabbatarianism was built on a long tradition of high Sabbath views in England, when it reached full bloom in Nicholas Bound it contained some important innovative Puritan elements, especially the dogmatic insistence on the divine institution of Sunday as the New Testament Sabbath. Similarly, anti-Sabbatarianism, although built upon a tradition of anti-Presbyterianism, was something of an Anglican innovation. This anti-Sabbatarianism drove Sabbatarianism completely into the Puritan camp and was equally responsible for the increasing polarization of English Protestantism in the seventeenth century. Its insistence upon reading Presbyterian motives into Sabbatarianism alienated an important and valuable part of the church, eventually to the point of removing that authentic element of Reformed Protestantism altogether. Sabbatarianism and anti-Sabbatarianism were both important factors in the development of two parties in the seventeenth-century Church of England that moved farther and farther away from each other as well as from the more moderating strains of Protestantism that had enabled them to coexist earlier. Although high Sabbath views were not initially Puritan, genuine Sabbatarianism went a step too far, and the strong anti-Sabbatarian reaction created a polarized situation in which Sabbatarianism, Puritanism, and Presbyterianism would become virtually interchangeable terms in the seventeenth century. Both Sabbatarianism and anti-Sabbatarianism were important movements in the series of events leading to the English civil war.

II

5

THE
THEOLOGICAL MATRIX
OF SABBATARIANISM

"IN THE NATURE OF THINGS," writes Jens Møller, "systematic theology is international."[1] In the sixteenth century, when there was a single western European theological language, Møller's law was especially valid. When the learned all read and wrote Latin, Babel—the greatest threat to international theology—must have seemed irrelevant.

The English Channel was not a great threat. English theology in the sixteenth century was not insular; it was European theology. It is easy to forget that the thought of the English Reformation—Puritan, Anglican, or whatever additional label is attached to it—was essentially Reformed, Protestant thought. The Church of England, for all the unique circumstances of its birth, was still basically the English extension of a supranational Protestantism. Whether expressed liturgically in the Book of Common Prayer or confessionally in the Thirty-nine Articles, the faith of the Church of England was the faith of the Continental Reformation.

On the large issues, there was an international theological vocabulary and widespread agreement on the meaning of the fundamental

---

[1]Jens Møller, "The Beginnings of Puritan Covenant Theology," *Journal of Ecclesiastical History* 14 (1963): 58.

concepts. Justification, faith, grace, election, sanctification, repentance, law, covenant—these were international Protestant doctrines. In this chapter we will focus on that larger theological context of English Sabbatarianism in an attempt to elucidate the rising tide of interest in the Decalogue in general and the fourth commandment in particular so evident in the late-sixteenth-century English church. We will use William Perkins as the model for how Sabbatarianism functioned within this larger theological framework.

Most Sabbatarian treatises were carefully hewn expositions of the fourth commandment. They were detailed, often tedious, exegetical analyses of Exodus 20:8-11. Many of them, moreover, appeared within larger studies of the Ten Commandments. Lancelot Andrewes, for example, dealt with the fourth commandment not by itself, but in a series of lectures on the Decalogue. In other words, concern for the Sabbath arose in the context of a broader interest in the Decalogue, which was viewed as a convenient summary of God's will for his people that was still relevant—in all of its dimensions—to Christian life in the sixteenth century. English Protestants were preoccupied with questions about moral life, and moral life, in their view, was simply a matter of obedience to the will of God expressed in the law.

This moral concern was not new in the closing part of the century. English reformers had been attuned to the dangers of Antinomianism from the beginning, and there is much early evidence of emphasis on good works in their theology. John Hooper, the fascinating mid-century forerunner of both Puritanism and Sabbatarianism, wrote a popular exposition of the Ten Commandments in 1548 that went through three editions and made some astonishing claims about the Decalogue. Hooper raised the Ten Commandments to a position of supreme importance in the Bible, asserting that they contain "the effect and whole sum of all the scripture! And whatsoever is said or written by the prophets, Christ, or the apostles, it is none other thing but the interpretation and exposition of these ten words or ten commandments." Through the Decalogue we learn "how to know God, to follow virtue, and to come to eternal life." Everything God would have us know is summarized therein, for "the heavenly God eternal hath concluded all the doctrine celestial in ten words or commandments."[2]

Similarly, in Thomas Becon's *Catechism* published in 1560, the law is given a prominent place and is treated at length.[3] Alexander Nowell's *Catechism* was another early, popular summary of Christian doctrine including an extensive section on the law. It was widely used since it was authorized by the Convocation of 1562 "for the bringing up of the youth in godliness, in the schools of the whole realm."[4] Even the early prayer-book liturgies highlighted the law and encouraged the development of moral theology. After each commandment, including the fourth, the worshiping community was to say, "Lord have mercy upon us and incline our hearts to keep this law." Sabbatarians later used this litany as an argument that the fourth commandment had always been regarded as morally binding in the Church of England.[5] In the writings of the earliest English reformers, it is not difficult to find abundant evidence of an emphasis on the intimate relationship between faith and works, and on the continuing need for the law as a guide for Christians and for the entire commonwealth. "Moral theology" in England is discernible as early as the 1540s.

This strong ethical concern with its keen interest in the law was not unique to England. Sixteenth-century English theology was essentially Reformed theology in the tradition of John Calvin. One of Calvin's greatest theological accomplishments was the inclusion of a significant place for law and good works within his theology of sovereign grace. Calvin countered Roman Catholic charges of an inherent Antinomianism in Protestant thought in at least three interrelated ways: by assigning the law a "third use"; by emphasizing human responsibility in the covenant of grace; and by a doctrine of sanctification so intimately tied to justification that the one cannot be considered apart from the other. The ultimate effect of all three was to raise the visibility of law in Reformed thought.

---

[2]John Hooper, *Early Writings* (Cambridge: Parker Society, 1843) 271-82.

[3]*Works of Thomas Becon* (Cambridge: Parker Society, 1844) 80-85.

[4]*Nowell's Catechism* (Cambridge: Parker Society, 1853) v.

[5]Peter Heylyn, *The History of the Sabbath*, 2:240; Robert Sanderson, *A Sovereigne Antidote* (London, 1636) 9-12.

The law functioned in Calvin's thought not only as the punitive instrument that reveals sin and hence drives the sinner to Christ or as the deterrent to restrain the sin of unredeemed people in fallen society, but also as the continuing guide for the Christian life.[6] He calls this third use of the law, in fact, the "principal use" of the law. The law is needed to teach and exhort the Christian in the way of the will of the Lord. Life in Christ is a life of love for God and neighbor, but love needs a guide. Love needs rules. That guide is the moral law, the will of God revealed throughout Scripture and summarized in the Decalogue. Since this is the norm for life in Christ, a life born in grace, the law does not conflict with grace. Although it is never a means *to* grace, the law, in Calvin's thought, virtually becomes a means *of* grace. As an indispensable aid to the new life in Christ, it is an instrument of freedom, not of bondage. Hence, the law achieves considerable prominence in Calvin's thought, and the Decalogue is given careful scrutiny in the *Institutes*, the *Commentaries*, and in his sermons. English Protestant attention to the law has its roots in the theology of Calvin.

In his essay "The Covenant of Grace in Calvin's Teaching," Anthony Hoekema shows that already in "Calvin's teachings on the covenant both the sovereign grace of God and the serious responsibility of man come into sharp and clear focus."[7] He argues that the covenant in Calvin's thought is the key to his understanding of the God-man relationship. Time and again, in his *Commentaries, Deuteronomy Sermons*, and also in the *Institutes*, Calvin stresses that "in all covenants of his mercy the Lord requires of his servants in return uprightness and sanctity of life, lest his goodness be mocked."[8] Uprightness and sanctity of life, of course, are defined by the law of God. The further development of "covenant theology" in England is well known. The doctrine of the covenant of grace, infused with a strong note of mu-

[6]John Calvin, *Institutes*, 2.7.6-12. Cf. I. John Hesselink, "Calvin's Concept and Use of the Law" (Th.D. diss., Basel, 1961); Ralph R. Sundquist, "The Third Use of the Law in the Thought of John Calvin" (Ph.D. diss., Columbia, 1970).

[7]Anthony Hoekema, "The Covenant of Grace in Calvin's Teaching," *Calvin Theological Journal* (November 1967): 133-61.

[8]Calvin, *Institutes*, 3.7.5. Cf. 2.10, 4.13; and *Commentary* on Gen. 17.

tuality, is discernible very early in English Reformed thought.[9] It is
prominent already in Tyndale and finds a place in the writings of both
Hooper and John Bradford about mid-century. Even more important,
the covenant doctrine is included in the notes of the Geneva Bible, first
published in 1560. Emphasis on the covenant gathered momentum as
the century wore on. Dudley Fenner expounded on the doctrine in his
Sacra Theologia in 1585, and the covenant is discernible in Cartwright's
thought, especially in *A Methodical Short Catechism*. Perkins was one of
the first in England to distinguish between a covenant of works and a
covenant of grace, and subsequently this distinction became standard
orthodoxy with a full-blown covenant theology developing in the seventeenth century. Already in the sixteenth century, however, the doctrine of the covenant was one of the important ways by which a special
ethical emphasis was introduced into Reformed theology in general and
English theology in particular. In this climate, the Decalogue—as the
"ten words of the covenant"—naturally received increased attention
and the Sabbath—as one of the primary means of nurturing covenant
life—likewise flourished.

A third theological emphasis that tended to tilt Calvin's thought in
the direction of intense moral concern is his emphasis on sanctification. For Calvin, the sanctified life is so tied up with justification that
the two are treated as different dimensions of the same doctrine. He
states, "As Christ cannot be torn into parts, so these two which we
perceive in him together and conjointly are inseparable—namely,
righteousness and sanctification."[10] In the *Institutes*, Calvin moves from
human faith response directly to a treatment of the Christian life in the
famous Golden Book.[11] Only after this challenge to holy living does
Calvin begin his exposition of justification. It is yet another way to
counter any tendencies toward moral carelessness that could arise from
the sovereign-grace emphasis in his thought. And once again, he de-

[9]Cf. Møller, "Beginnings of Puritan Covenant Theology," 46; Michael
McGiffert, "Grace and Works: The Rise and Division of Covenant Divinity in
Elizabethan Puritanism," *Harvard Theological Review* 75:4 (1982): 463-502; and
George Marsden, "Perry Miller's Rehabilitation of the Puritans," *Church His-
tory* 39 (March 1970) 97ff.

[10]Calvin, *Institutes*, 3.11.6.

[11]Ibid., 3.vi-x.

fines the sanctified life in terms of obedience to the will of God expressed in the law. Calvin practiced what he preached. English
reformers who settled in Geneva during the Marian exile had the opportunity to witness this sanctification theology in action. Ecclesiasti-
cally, he established new machinery for the control of morals in Geneva
through the office of lay elder and the work of the consistory.[12] Surely
the moral discipline we especially associate with English Puritanism
was learned, at least in part, on the Continent. And in the Sabbath
doctrine the sanctification emphasis is overwhelming.

These three strands of Calvin's thought provided the broader context in which moral theology in general, and Sabbatarianism in particular, flourished. The three are interrelated of course. The covenant is
the arrangement by which God and his people live in a dynamic historical relationship and in which human beings have clear reciprocal
obligations. Sanctification stresses growth in man's covenant life. The
law is the instrument of the covenant that guides the new, sanctified
life in Christ in the way of the will of God. It was within this framework that English moral theology was constructed in the later sixteenth century, and such moral theology provided the immediate
context for the development of Sabbatarianism.

There is yet another issue of intense practical and theological concern in the late sixteenth century that is intimately tied to English piety
and moral theology: the quest for personal assurance of salvation. In
Reformed thought, God and sovereign grace are supreme themes. In
the beginning God created a world designed for one grand end—to
manifest his glory. He never withdrew from that which he created, and
he continues to govern its history. Given such a starting point, the entrance of sin into the world is a mystery, but the presence of sin and
its results is nonetheless a stark reality. The Fall was a total disaster,
casting humankind into the darkness of alienation from God where the
human condition is utterly hopeless. Deliverance is possible only
through the sovereign, holy, powerful, and gracious work of God. Redemption is promised early in the Scriptures. It is wholly, totally of God,
for it flows ultimately from his free grace and sovereign will. The his-

---

[12]Ibid., 4.12. Cf. R. N. Caswell, "Calvin's View of Ecclesiastical Discipline,"
in *John Calvin*, ed. Gervase E. Duffield (Grand Rapids: Eerdmans, 1966) 210-
26.

torical reality of that deliverance is initiated by God's eternal, unconditioned choice. This predestined salvation is called "election."

But not all are saved, and that sad statement leads us into the murkier side of Reformed thought. There are already signs in Calvin's *Institutes* that a problem might develop, especially at the point of introducing the prospect of nondeliverance or reprobation. If *all* are saved by the sovereign power and love of God, no questions need be asked. But if some are not saved in a world that begins and ends with God, questions about the nature of this God are bound to be raised, as well as questions about humanity's role in the whole process of election and reprobation. Are human beings but helpless pawns whose eternal destiny is capriciously determined by an unpredictable and arbitrary divine disposition? Or is genuine significance to be found in human faith and unbelief, in piety and impiety? Furthermore, if election and reprobation are decrees that are established in the mystery of eternity, how can anyone be personally assured of salvation? Must not life be lived in precarious uncertainty under the Damoclean sword of predestination?

Calvin developed his theology in such a way that the force of these problems was somewhat blunted. His treatment of divine election, for example, comes relatively late in his theology, and it comes in the context of soteriological discussion, only after a lengthy and profound treatment of faith, justification, and sanctification. This order of thought serves to place more emphasis on God's love as a central, defining feature of his sovereignty, and on the need for and significance of the historical human response in the dynamics of salvation. It lessens the possibility of a cold, sovereign determinism in which human response is irrelevant and God's love questionable. In fact, Calvin's theology in general, beginning as it does with a correlative emphasis on God and mankind, leaves considerable room for a dynamic, covenantal interaction between the divine and the human in history. Moreover, Calvin's definition of faith incorporates the doctrine of personal assurance. He does not make a distinction between true faith and assurance, but defines faith as "a firm and certain knowledge of God's benevolence toward us, founded upon the truth of the freely given promise in Christ, both revealed in our minds and sealed upon our hearts through the

Holy Spirit."[13] Calvin freely admits that this assured faith is always ac-
companied by some doubt—sometimes severe doubts. Yet Calvin
himself did not become as deeply enmeshed in the nagging pastoral
problem of eternal security as did his followers.

A theological shift of considerable importance occurred within Reformed Protestant thought in the second half of the sixteenth century.
This shift is already apparent in the theology of Theodore Beza, Calvin's successor in Geneva, who adopted a system of thought that nearly
all Reformed theologians, including those in England, would subsequently follow.[14] Beza removed the doctrine of predestination from the
soteriological context in which Calvin had considered it, and positioned
it where it would exercise more prominence within and control over the
entire theological system. He moved it up front to occupy a place
within the doctrine of God and his pre-creational, eternal decrees. Now
the specter of determinism threatened with new intensity. People raised
urgent questions about the freedom and significance of human faith response to God and about God's precise relationship to election and especially to reprobation.[15] Moreover, in Beza's thought, the bond
between faith and assurance was weakened. While he also included
assurance in his definition of faith, he did not emphasize as strongly
as Calvin the internal testimony of the Spirit and the role of Christ as
the mirror and pledge of our election. Rather he encouraged the active
pursuit of assurance by means of a "practical syllogism": those who

---

[13]Calvin, *Institutes*, 3.2.7. Cf. Dewey Wallace, *Puritans and Predestination*
(Chapel Hill: University of North Carolina Press, 1982).

[14]Basil Hall, "Calvin against the Calvinists," *John Calvin*, 19-37; Robert T.
Kendall, *Calvin and English Calvinism to 1649* (New York: Oxford University
Press, 1979). Chap. 2 deals specifically with Beza. See also Philip C. Holtrop,
"The Bolsec Controversy" (Ph.D. diss., Harvard, 1988). Other unpublished
materials by Dr. Holtrop, Calvin College, are also especially helpful here. Ken-
dall's book has sparked a vigorous reaction. See Paul Helm, *Calvin and the Cal-
vinists* (Carlisle PA: Banner of Truth, 1982); W. Stanford Reid in *Westminster
Theological Journal* 43 (1980): 155-64; Tony Lane, "The Quest for the Historical
Calvin," *Evangelical Quarterly* 55 (April 1983).

[15]At Cambridge these questions were raised in the Barrett and Baro contro-
versies in the 1590s. On these proto-arminian controversies, see Tyacke, *Anti-
Calvinists* (Oxford: Clarendon Press, 1987) and Harry C. Porter, *Reformation and
Reaction in Tudor Cambridge* (Cambridge: at the University Press, 1958).

are elect perform good works; I perform good works; therefore I am elect.[16] Beza laid the groundwork for a more cognitive, empirical approach to assurance involving an examination of the sanctified life. The norm or touchstone of sanctification, of course, is to be found in the law, summarized in the Decalogue. And just as the law is the norm of piety, so it is conversely the mirror of sin. Beza therefore also stressed the law as the key element in preparation for faith. The first use of the law, he says, is to show us our sin, to "make us sorry, and be humble and throw down ourselves to the uttermost." Just as "the colour of black is never better set forth than when white is set by it, so the spirit of God beginneth by the preaching of the law."[17] So the law began to achieve more and more importance in the Reformed tradition, functioning as the key both to preparation for faith and the assurance of faith.

The growing concern about personal assurance is also evident in the Heidelberg theologians, Ursinus and Zanchius. It was Ursinus, for example, who wrote that "a good conscience is a certain knowledge, that we have faith," and who further defined conscience as "nothing else" but a "practical syllogism" in the mind.[18] Zanchius heavily stressed the "effects" of election in a Christian's life that bring him assurance of salvation. The result of this emphasis was to encourage introspection through the practical syllogism. God has given us "seals" of election, "namely in printing in us a lively form and image of God, foreknowing us, loving us, electing us." We "may behold in ourselves some sure representations of all these imprinted, and even stamped in us by the word: and so by the beholding of these forms and impressions in ourselves, we shall easily be brought to the knowledge of those patterns, (as it were) which are in the Lord himself." With justification comes "sanctification, and renovation of life, a good conscience, love not feigned, a pure heart and clean, patience in adversity, and boasting in tribulation, all good works and fruits of the spirit." By these a person "must needs be persuaded of his election: for God only doth

---

[16]Kendall, *Calvin and English Calvinism*, 33ff. Beza addressed the issue of personal assurance in a treatise well known in England, *A Briefe and Pithie Summe of the Christian Faith* (London, 1563).

[17]Quoted in Kendall, *Calvin and English Calvinism*, 37.

[18]Quoted ibid., 40.

communicate these unto the elect."[19] Doing good works is clearly the
primary means to "make our election and calling sure." It is in fact "one
of the chiefest uses of good works, that by them, not as by causes, but
as by effects of predestination and faith, both we, and also our neigh-
bours are certified of our election, and of our salvation too."[20]

In England, the appearance of this "experimental Predestinarianism" with its overwhelming concern about the quest for personal assurance of election corresponds almost precisely with the efflorescence
of Sabbatarianism. Richard Greenham, William Perkins, Richard Rogers, John Dod, Robert Cleaver, William Bradshaw, Stephen Egerton,
Arthur Hildersam, William Gouge, Samuel Ward, Paul Baynes, Richard Sibbes, Robert Bolton, and John Preston were late-sixteenth-century or early-seventeenth-century pastors with a burning desire to help
their parishioners achieve personal assurance by examining the sanctified life defined by the law of God. Richard Rogers speaks typically
when, on the opening page of his well-known *Seven Treatises*, he declares that the issue of personal assurance is "the weightiest and chiefest point of all others in divinity."[21] The title of Perkins's first casuistic
treatise similarly reveals the deep concern about personal assurance:
*A Case of Conscience, the Greatest That Ever Was: How a Man May Know
Whether He is the Childe of God or No.* In this treatise the practical syllogism, with the Decalogue at its core, receives crystal-clear expression.
Perkins appeals over and over again to the keeping of God's commandments as the sure route to personal assurance. Almost without
exception, discussions about personal assurance led to analyses of the
Ten Commandments as the norm for the sanctified life.

William Perkins, the first Puritan systematic theologian, provides
the clearest example of how the Sabbath in particular and the Decalogue in general functioned within the larger framework of English Reformed theology. As I have already indicated, the Sabbath makes an

[19]*A Brief Discourse Taken Out of the Writings of Her. Zanchius* (London, 1595)
31.

[20]Ibid., 42.

[21]Richard Rogers, *Seven Treatises* (London, 1603) 1.

early appearance in *A Golden Chaine* when Perkins discusses the doctrine of creation. It appears, however, at a most surprising point—not in connection with God's creative work ending in Sabbath rest, but in a chapter entitled "Of Man, and the Estate of Innocency." Human beings in their pre-Fall perfection possessed a number of important characteristics, says Perkins, one of which was subjection to God. In this subjection, "man was bound to perform obedience to the commandments of God: which were two. The one was concerning the two trees: the other, the observation of the Sabbath."[22]

In this remarkable passage, Perkins sets the Sabbath in a position of enormous theological significance. It is placed squarely in the center of covenant life with God. Perkins, who was one of the first to distinguish a covenant of works from the covenant of grace, does not speak explicitly of a works covenant here—that will come a bit later—but the necessary ingredients are present, and Sabbath keeping is one of its explicit conditions. So the Sabbath is set in a legal, covenantal, ethical context.

Perkins goes on to explain how he gleans from the Genesis passage this commandment to observe the Sabbath in addition to the commandment regarding the trees in the garden. He writes, "God's commandment concerning the observation of the Sabbath, is that, by which God ordained the sanctification of the Sabbath. Genesis 2.3. *God blessed the seventh day, and sanctified it.*"[23] Perkins hereby furnishes the biblical rationale for exalting the fourth commandment above all the others and for placing it at the center of the Christian's moral life. And although Perkins does not go on to make Sabbath breaking a prominent element in Adam's fall, yet by introducing the Sabbath as one of only two pre-Fall commands, he provides theological justification for making Sabbath breaking one of the more heinous sins. Further comment about the Sabbath, however, does not appear at this early juncture. Perkins postpones elaborating on it until much later in his lengthy section on the Decalogue.

The precise point at which Perkins introduces the Decalogue must be noted with care because its placement says much about Puritan the-

---

[22]Perkins, *A Golden Chaine*, 20.

[23]Ibid., 21.

ology. It is deliberately and explicitly placed in the context of election!
Predestination had been discussed earlier in the introduction to *A
Golden Chaine* as the eternal decree from which all of human history
proceeds. Perkins discusses election as one of the two aspects of predestination, not with emphasis on election as the eternal decree of God,
but rather on its "execution" in history and in the life of mankind: "The
execution of this decree, is an action, by which God, even as he pur-
posed with himself, worketh all those things, which he decreed for the
salvation of the elect. For they whom God elected to this end, that they
should inherit eternal life, were also elected to these subordinate means,
whereby, as by steps, they might attain this end, and without which,
it were impossible to obtain it."[24] The concepts of covenant and law are
designated as the "subordinate means" by which the decree of election is historically executed. This theological placement of covenant and
law is perfectly in keeping with the use of the law in the practical syllogism to secure personal assurance of election.

Perkins's discussion of the Decalogue, and hence of the Sabbath, is
an integral part of his discussion of the covenant. First, he defines covenant in general as God's "contract with man, concerning life eternal,
upon certain conditions." It consists of two parts: "God's promise to
man, man's promise to God."[25] Perkins's initial statement on the covenant is strongly conditional: "God's promise to man, is that, whereby
he bindeth himself to man to be his God, if he break not the condition.
Man's promise to God, is that, whereby he voweth his allegiance unto
his Lord, and to perform the condition between them." This explicit
reference to conditions in the covenant is noteworthy because it signals a shift from original Calvinism. This new development is related
to the important distinction Perkins makes between the covenant of
works and the covenant of grace. "The covenant of works, is God's
covenant, made with the condition of perfect obedience, and is expressed in the moral law." So it is initially in the covenant of works
that the Decalogue finds its significance, for the Decalogue is "an
abridgement of the whole law, and the covenant of works."[26] Here

[24]Ibid., 38.

[25]Ibid., 59.

[26]Ibid., 60.

Perkins alludes to Exodus 34:27, which refers to the Ten Commandments as the "words of the covenant." Clearly Perkins regards the Decalogue and the covenant of works as essentially one and the same.

One might conclude from this identification of the Ten Commandments with the covenant of works that the Decalogue would not be important in Perkins's view of the Christian life in the covenant of grace. But this is by no means the case. The law plays both a preparatory role leading into the covenant of grace as well as an educational role within the life of grace.

A theology of preparation for grace is perceptible in Perkins. In a brief chapter on the use of the law, he speaks first of a threefold use "in unregenerate persons." These uses are to "lay open sin, and make it known"; to actually "effect and augment sin" since sinners ordinarily are inclined to do that which is prohibited; and finally, to reveal the penalty of eternal damnation for breaking the law "without offering any hope of pardon." All of these uses are designed to help bring unregenerate people to Christ. "If therefore, thou desirest seriously eternal life: first take a narrow examination of thyself, and the course of thy life, by the square of God's law: then set before thine eyes the curse that is due unto sin, that, thus bewailing thy misery, and despairing utterly of thine own power, to attain everlasting happiness, thou mayest renounce thyself, and be provoked to seek and sue unto Christ Jesus."[27] So the law functions to reveal our sin and need for the covenant of grace.

But this by no means exhausts the uses of the law. It applies also to the lives of God's people within the covenant of grace itself, "for it guideth them to new obedience in the whole course of their life, which obedience may be acceptable to God by Christ." Perkins bases this additional use of the law, corresponding to Calvin's third use, on Romans 3:31, "Do we therefore through faith make the Law of none effect? God forbid: nay we rather establish the law." He also refers for support to the praises of the law sung by God's people in Psalm 119. So Perkins, though his emphasis falls on the Decalogue as a summary of the covenant of works, also connects his interpretation of the Deca-

---

[27]Ibid., 166. Cf. Norman Pettit, *The Heart Prepared* (New Haven: Yale University Press, 1966) 61ff.

logue to the covenant of grace, hence making it supremely relevant to the New Testament Christian community.[28]

Perkins defines the covenant of grace as "that whereby God freely promising Christ, and his benefits, exacteth again of man, that he would by faith receive Christ, and repent of his sins."[29] He mentions that "in this covenant we do not offer much, and promise small to God, but in a manner do only receive: even as the last will and testament of a man, is not for the testator's, but the heir's commodity." When, therefore, the commandments are viewed in the context of the covenant of grace, they are no longer conditional demands but rather a description of the living, covenant relationship between God and his redeemed people. As such, they provide indispensable aid and guidance for the cultivation of that relationship.

The Sabbath commandment plays a role of key significance in the nurture of the covenant relationship. It establishes a "holy time consecrated to the worship and glorifying of God."[30] Faith is crucial in the covenant of grace, and faith comes through preaching and the sacraments. For Perkins it is precisely the Sabbath that "preserveth and conserveth the ministry of the word, and the solemn worship of God, especially in the assemblies of the Church. And in this respect we are upon this day, as well enjoined a rest from our vocations, as the Jews were."[31] Moreover, the Sabbath provides a time for working out the other commandments. While physical rest is a fringe benefit of the day, this rest is primarily designed to provide opportunity for the "performing of those spiritual works, which are commanded in the second and third commandment." To rise early for proper self-preparation, to "be present at public assemblies" in order to hear the Word, participate in the sacraments, and "celebrate the Name of the Lord," and "to

[28]Ibid., 62. After Perkins, even more stress was laid on the law as a part of the covenant of grace. Henry Burton speaks of a "Covenant of grace made to us in Christ under which the law is given" and regards this as an "invincible arguement" for the "perpetual morality of the sabbath." *The Law and the Gospell Reconciled* (London, 1631) 24, 26.

[29]Ibid., 166.

[30]Ibid., 98.

[31]Ibid., 103.

spend the rest of the sabbath in the meditation of God's word, and his creatures," as well as to perform works of charity—these are the "spiritual works" of the Sabbath.[32] Since it involves such fundamentals as hearing the Word and performing works of mercy, there was no other "subordinate means" that could outstrip the Sabbath in importance in the execution of the decree of election.

In a theology whose keynotes were grace and predestination, the teachings of the covenant, law, and sanctified life found a special place and meaning in late-sixteenth-century Reformed Calvinism. The law became increasingly important to prepare for grace, as a guide for grace, and to achieve assurance of grace. And so, perhaps especially in England, the theological emphasis began to shift subtly from election to the elected, from the eternal decrees to the historical covenant, and from justification to sanctification. The emphasis in English Reformed thought at the close of the sixteenth century was on the good life as the effect of election, the means of election, and the proof of election. Protestantism, particularly in this post-Tridentine period, was under some pressure to fill the moral vacuum created by its emphasis on justification by grace through faith alone. English Calvinists took the lead in doing so. Cambridge theologians were not out of touch with the people. Ordinary village parishioners needed moral direction (as the Dedham minutes so clearly indicate), and the theological leaders were determined to give it to them without sacrificing, if at all possible, the Protestant universe of grace. In the moral theology that developed, it was natural that the Decalogue should come to be interpreted and applied with rigor and in great detail.

In this climate of renewed interest in the Decalogue and its application to the Christian life, the Sabbath flourished. Keeping the Sabbath was particularly attractive in this time of concern about maintaining the moral life without sacrificing a high doctrine of predestination. The end and purpose of the Sabbath corresponded precisely with the historical means and effects of election: the call to Christ through the hearing of the Word, the challenge to faith, the need for sanctification, the "love of righteousness and detestation of sin," the

---

[32]Ibid., 103, 104.

care and endeavor to do good works, and the prayers to God for aid in the battle against the world, the flesh, and the devil. Both by providing a setting for the calling of the Christian through the Word of God, and by the encouragement of a good life of devotion to God and service to mankind, the Sabbath found an integral place in the experimental Predestinarianism of the late sixteenth century.

6

SABBATARIAN APPEALS
TO THE CONTINENT

ENGLISH SABBATARIANS did not claim originality for their views, not even for the position that became the pivotal element of the Puritan Sabbath, Sunday absolutism. After the consensus on the Sabbath broke down in the 1580s when Sabbath theology and practice moved into the spotlight of ecclesiastical debate, the Sabbatarians were eager to show that they had a veritable cloud of witnesses supporting their position. They appealed to a vast array of ancient, medieval, and especially Continental Reformed authorities for support.

Such appeals to the Continent had became commonplace, for the English Reformation was by no means an insular movement. English churchmen were listening and learning on the Continent as early as the 1530s, and Continental theologians like Martin Bucer and Peter Martyr were teaching in England in the 1540s. During the reign of the Catholic Queen Mary in the 1550s, droves of English Protestants fled to havens across the Channel, especially Geneva, Zurich, Strassbourg, and Frankfurt. There they were marinated in the strong juices of the "best Reformed churches on the continent." Oxford and Cambridge libraries were lined with tomes from Continental theologians, and in English religious treatises there was consistent and persistent appeal both to classical and medieval thinkers like Irenaeus, Justin Martyr, Jerome, Chrysostom, Athanasius, Augustine, Aquinas, and to sixteenth-century contemporaries, especially Calvin, Bullinger, Bucer, Beza, Ramus, Peter Martyr, Zanchius, Junius, Musculus, and Tremellius.

In most of the early Sabbatarian treatises such appeals are sprin-
kled here and there in the body of the text; but in the landmark books
on the fourth commandment written by Nicholas Bound, there is a
more carefully arranged marginal apparatus.[1] In the 1595 edition most
of his citations come from the works of John Calvin. In the 1606 edition
the references to Calvin are exceeded only by references to Jerome
Zanchius. Evidently between 1595 and 1606 Bound acquainted himself
with the distinctive Sabbath views of Zanchius, for there are no Zanchius quotes in the 1595 edition.

Were these appeals to Continental reformers legitimate? Was there
a developing Sabbatarianism on the Continent parallel to that in
England? To what extent can the distinguishing marks of Sabbatarianism—the perpetual, moral significance of the fourth commandment, strict Sabbath observance, and above all, Sunday absolutism—
be found in the views of the reformers to whom the Sabbatarians appealed? In an effort to answer these questions, we will explore the Sabbath views of a number of reformers, with special emphasis on Calvin
and Zanchius.[2]

Most of Bound's references to Calvin are to the Deuteronomy sermons, especially sermons 34 and 35, Calvin's two sermons on the fourth
commandment. There are also a number of appeals to the *Commentaries.*
Bound cites Calvin's commentaries on Genesis 2:3, Exodus 20:8 and 34:21,
Leviticus 25:20, Numbers 15:32, Psalm 32:2, Jeremiah 17:27, John 5:17, and
Acts 1:11. He uses references to the commentaries, however, in the context of making relatively minor points in his Sabbatarian argument.

It is not only interesting but highly significant that there are no references whatsoever to Calvin's *Institutes* in any of the Sabbatarian literature, even though this landmark theological work was well known
and widely used at Cambridge and was even available in the English
language.[3] For the purposes of this discussion, it is important never-

---

[1]Nicholas Bound, *The Doctrine of the Sabbath* (London, 1595); idem, *Sabbathum Veteris* (London, 1606).

[2]Cf. John H. Primus, "Calvin and the Puritan Sabbath," in *Exploring the
Heritage of John Calvin* (Grand Rapids: Baker, 1976) 40-75; Richard Gaffin, *Calvin
and the Sabbath* (Master's thesis, Westminster Seminary, 1962).

[3]The Thomas Norton translation was first published in 1561 with at least
five later editions before 1595.

theless to include a careful consideration of the Sabbath material in the *Institutes*, for it is here that Calvin gives the most thorough exposition of his Sabbath theology. A consideration of this material will also make it quite clear why the Sabbatarians chose to ignore it. On the other hand, a careful consideration of the Deuteronomy sermons will reveal why Bound appeals to them with such regularity.

The best source for Calvin's theology of the Sabbath is book 2, chapter 8 of the *Institutes*, where Calvin offers his exposition of the Ten Commandments. Most of this material comes from the 1537 edition,and it appears there was very little subsequent development in Calvin's Sabbath theology. There are, moreover, no substantial additions to that theology in the numerous references to the Sabbath scattered throughout the rest of Calvin's works.

In the *Institutes*, Calvin's opening statement on the fourth commandment reveals his fundamental theme. "The purpose of this commandment is that, being dead to our own inclinations and works, we should meditate on the Kingdom of God, and that we should practice this meditation in the ways established by him."[4] In the phrase "being dead to our own inclinations and works," Calvin's fundamental theological keynote—*grace*—is implicit. His interpretation of the fourth commandment is governed and controlled by that theme. Salvation is the gracious act of a sovereign God. The Sabbath is given as a reminder of this grace, for it calls us to rest from our own works. In Calvin's view, the call to a Sabbath rest is a call to abandon completely human works as a basis for a renewed relationship to God, a relationship grounded in grace.

Calvin immediately goes on to state that "this commandment has a particular consideration distinct from the others," thereby calling for a "different order of exposition." Sabbatarians also believed in the uniqueness of the fourth commandment, but Calvin finds this uniqueness in something the Sabbatarians consistently denied: the ceremo-

---

[4]This citation and those that follow in this portion of the chapter, unless otherwise noted, are from the *Institutes*, ed. John T. McNeill (Philadelphia: Westminster Press, 1960) bk. 2, chap. 8, pp. 394-401.

nial character of the fourth commandment.[5] He agrees with the early fathers who "called this commandment a foreshadowing because it contains the outward keeping of a day, which, upon Christ's coming, was abolished with the other figures." In fact, for Calvin, this ceremonial foreshadowing "occupied the chief place in the Sabbath." Calvin clearly affirms a strong ceremonial element in the fourth commandment that was fulfilled and abrogated by the coming of Jesus Christ.

However, there is more to Calvin's view of the Sabbath than the ceremonial dimension. In addition, there are two elements that must be continually observed by the Christian community throughout all time: a provision for communal worship, and a command to give a day of rest to those who are under the authority of others. The paragraph outlining his three-dimensional view of the fourth commandment deserves quotation in full.

> First, under the repose of the seventh day the heavenly Law-giver meant to represent to the people of Israel spiritual rest, in which believers ought to lay aside their own works to allow God to work in them. Secondly, he meant that there was to be a stated day for them to assemble to hear the law and perform the rites, or at least to devote it particularly to meditation upon his works, and thus through this remembrance to be trained in piety. Thirdly, he resolved to give a day of rest to servants and those who are under the authority of others, in order that they should have some respite from toil.

Calvin then returns to the first of the three elements, the foreshadowing of spiritual rest that is of primary importance in his Sabbath theology. He cites evidence of the great emphasis on this commandment and the requirement of absolute obedience to it throughout the Old Testament era. The implication of Calvin's stress on the strict Old Testament observance is that in Christ "the spiritual rest" element of the Sabbath was fulfilled so that consequently there is a diminished emphasis on precise Sabbath observance in the New Testament. Al-

---

[5]Kenneth Parker says that Calvin "attempted to interpret the sabbath precept in a manner which excluded the moral-ceremonial categories established by the scholastics" (*The English Sabbath*, 27). But this is hardly the case. Calvin consistently uses the ceremonial category, distinguishing that aspect of the commandment from those aspects that are "perpetual" in it. This would appear to be tantamount to the ceremonial-moral distinction.

though the outward sign of the strict observance of a particular day has been abolished by Christ, the "inward reality" of the Sabbath remains for the Christian community of the New Testament era and for all time. This "inward reality" is at root the reality of grace. Calvin asserts, "We must be wholly at rest that God may work in us; we must yield our will; we must resign our heart; we must give up all our fleshly desires. In short, we must rest from all activities of our own contriving, so that, having God working in us, we may repose in him as the apostle also teaches." The rest and repose Calvin speaks of here, however, is a perpetual duty for the Christian, not restricted to one day in seven. It is a redemptive rest, an "eternal cessation," which for the Jews was represented by the observance of the Sabbath day.

In his Deuteronomy sermon 35, Calvin asserts—in marked contrast to the Sabbatarians—that since the Sabbath is in essence a sign of spiritual, redemptive rest for God's people, the fourth commandment is not universally applicable to all mankind. It is a sign for sanctified people, a sign of God's covenant relationship. "God saith, I have given you the Sabbath day to be as a sign that I make you holy, and that I am your God who reigneth among you. This is not common to all mortal men. For God granteth not such grace and privilege to the paynims and infidels, as to make them holy. He speaks but only to the people whom he adopted and chose to be his heritage."[6] Calvin underscores this argument by stating that the Sabbath is a "sign of God's separating of his faithful Church from all the rest of the world."

By the ceremonial element of the Sabbath, Calvin apparently is referring to the strict Jewish observance of a particular day each week as a representation of redemptive, eternal repose in God. Since this redemptive rest—symbolized by the Sabbath day in the history of Israel—finds its fulfillment in Christ, the external observance as a redemptive symbol is abolished in Christ. In the *Institutes* Calvin says emphatically, "He is, I say, the true fulfillment of the Sabbath." What in the old order was represented by the observance of one day in seven, now in the new order is represented by the living Christ—namely spiritual life and redemptive repose in God. Calvin concludes his interpretation of the first meaning of the Sabbath with this exhortation:

---

[6]*The Sermons of M. Iohn Caluin upon the Fifth Booke of Moses Called Deuteronomie,* trans. Arthur Golding (London, 1583) 207.

"Christians ought therefore to shun completely the superstitious observance of days." By "superstitious observance of days," he apparently means the keeping of holy days as a means of salvation. We now
find our eternal rest in Christ, not in a holy day.

The other two elements of the Sabbath commandment, however,
are not abrogated but are applicable to all times. The first of these is the
cultic element. By setting aside a day from the rest of the week, the
fourth commandment conveniently provides time for communal worship. The commandment itself does not explicitly require this, of
course, but Calvin argues that God's Word in other places makes it quite
clear that God's people are enjoined to assemble regularly for worship.
Calvin raises a very practical question: "But how can such meetings be
held unless they have been established and have their stated days?"
An ecclesiastical schedule must be established. All things must be done
decently and in order. If there is no "arrangement and regulation" to
set aside some specific time for worship, "immediate confusion and
ruin threaten the church." The need of the ancient Israelites for such
regulation was one of the reasons God established the Sabbath. And
Calvin adds, since Christians are subject to the same necessity as the
Jews in ancient times, Christians should continue to observe the Sabbath institution. He states, "For our most provident and merciful Father willed to see to our needs not less than those of the Jews." Calvin
develops this second element of the Sabbath commandment, then, in
the context of the practical need for good order in the church.

Calvin goes on to suggest that in a perfect world God's people would
meet daily for worship "so as to remove all distinction of days." But
this world is fallen, and the second element of the fourth commandment represents God's acknowledgment of human weakness. Calvin
makes a remarkable statement about the divine concession to human
sin and frailty: "But if the weakness of many made it impossible for
daily meetings to be held, and the rule of love does not allow more to
be required of them, why should we not obey the order we see laid
upon us by God's will?" To set aside a day a week for worship would,
of course, involve the risk of appearing to observe a "distinction of
days." But that risk must be taken. In fact, Calvin's Geneva was criticized for the practice of a Jewish "observance of days," an indication
that a "Lord's Day" was quite strictly observed there. Calvin defends
Genevan practice by arguing that although the observance of the Sab-

bath continues, the reason for and spirit of this observance have radically changed in the New Testament church. Christians no longer observe the Sabbath "as a ceremony with the most rigid scrupulousness, supposing a spiritual mystery to be figured thereby." Instead, they use it "as a remedy needed to keep order in the church." Sheer practical necessity requires cessation of labor on the Sabbath. Calvin distinguishes between a "distinction of days," which he opposes, and the "lawful selection that serves the peace of the Christian fellowship," which he supports. The Jewish Sabbath was abandoned by the early Christian community to overthrow superstition, and yet another day for worship was selected "because it was necessary to maintain decorum, order, and peace in the church." On this point the English anti-Sabbatarians could more legitimately appeal to Calvin than could the Sabbatarians.

The day set aside by the early Christians for the day of worship was Sunday, the first day of the week. Is there something special about that day, something that makes it inherently a better day for worship than the other days? Is it a day established by divine authority? Calvin answers the first question by stating that the first day of the week is peculiarly appropriate for worship because it was the day when the Lord arose, and "the purpose and fulfillment of that true rest" is ultimately to be found in Christ's Resurrection. "Hence, by the very day that brought the shadows to an end, Christians are warned not to cling to the shadow rite." In his commentary on Exodus 20:8, Calvin speaks of a "peculiar excellency in the Sabbath." But the context allows interpretation of "the Sabbath" in this quotation as Sabbath rest rather than as a specific day superior to other days. In his Deuteronomy sermon 34, Calvin alludes to the primary reason early Christians changed the day, but he does not stress the specific day to which it was changed. He argues that the day was changed after Christ's Resurrection to show that we have been freed from ceremonial bondage to the observance of days in the old order.

In a decidedly non-Sabbatarian passage, Calvin states explicitly that the church is neither bound to the first day by divine authority nor absolutely bound to the rhythm of one day in seven. He writes, "Nor do I cling to the number 'seven' so as to bind the church in subjection to it. And I shall not condemn churches that have other solemn days for their meetings, provided there be no superstition."[7] Later he criticizes the legalistic "fixing of one day in seven." In his commentary on Exodus 20:8, Calvin further addresses the question of the one-in-seven rhythm. Why, he asks, did God assign every seventh day as the Sabbath rather than the sixth or the tenth? In the course of his argument, Calvin links the one-in-seven rhythm to God's creation-rest pattern in Genesis 1. This does not mean Calvin thinks of the fourth commandment as a creation ordinance. Rather, he seems to say that when God gave the Israelites the Decalogue, a model for the fourth commandment was available, namely, his own creation activity. God selected that rhythm and introduced it into the fourth commandment. Calvin states, "I do not, however, doubt but that God created the world in six days and rested on the seventh, that He might give a manifestation of the perfect excellency of His works, and thus, proposing Himself as the model for our imitation, He signifies that He calls His own people to the true goal of felicity." Later, in his comments on the words "for in six days the Lord made heaven and earth . . . and rested on the seventh day," Calvin notes, "From this passage it may be probably conjectured that the hallowing of the Sabbath was prior to the Law." In the book of Exodus, Moses' injunction prohibiting the gathering of manna on the seventh day appears earlier than the Decalogue itself. But again, Calvin falls short of supporting the view that the fourth commandment was a creation ordinance. He only says that the observance of the seventh day of rest "seems to have had its origin from a well-known and received custom."

When, then, was the Sabbath first instituted? Calvin tentatively offers this possibility: it was probably established "when God revealed the rite of sacrifice to the Holy Fathers." By "holy Fathers," Calvin apparently means the Jewish patriarchs. He concludes, "But what in the depravity of human nature was altogether extinct among heathen nations, and almost obsolete with the race of Abraham, God renewed in His Law."

In his commentary on Genesis 3:2, Calvin appears to contradict his insistence in the *Institutes* that the church is not bound today to the one-

---

[7]John Pocklington reports that in Calvin's Geneva, there was talk of switching the day of worship from Sunday to Thursday, *Sunday No Sabbath* (London, 1636) 8.

in-seven rhythm.[8] In the Genesis commentary he stresses God's creation-rest pattern as the foundation for the requirement of "every seventh day" as a day of rest and worship for God's people. The apparent contradiction is easily resolved, however, when one takes account of another of Calvin's emphases: that one day in seven for worship is a *minimal* requirement. He argues several times that ideally we should assemble every day for worship, but because of our sloth and weakness we fail to do this. To ensure that some time will be set aside in mankind's busy schedule, God makes this minimal requirement. When Calvin, therefore, states in the *Institutes* that the church is not bound to the number seven and that Christians may have "other solemn days for their meetings," he simply means he would not object at all if the worship-and-work pattern were other than it is. He makes this explicit in his Deuteronomy sermon 34: "But yet must we observe the same order of having some day in the week, be it one or be it two, for that is left to the free choice of Christians."[9]

Obviously, then, the Christian community is not tied absolutely to the one-in-seven routine. God provided this command simply out of concern for establishing some order for his people. In setting up that order, God had to select some number. One in seven was natural and convenient because it follows God's own Creation rhythm. Thus, God, by his own example, allures humankind to keep at least one day in seven. If the people should choose to worship more often than this, they should do so. It is worth noting, in conclusion, that the Deuteronomy sermons—in which Calvin stresses one day in seven as the minimal requirement—were preached in worship gatherings on Thursday, 20 June and on Friday, 21 June 1555, not on the seventh day or on the first day of the week.

---

[8]Several have commented on and attempted to resolve this seeming contradiction. See Abraham Kuyper, *Tractaat van den Sabbath* (Amsterdam: J. A. Wormser, 1890) 81ff.; Louis Praamsma, "Calvijn over de Sabbath," *Church and Nation* 6 (28 Nov. 1961) 91-92; Gaffin, "Calvin and the Sabbath," 95ff. But they fail to note the significance of Calvin's emphasis on one day in seven as the *minimum* for worship.

[9]Golding, Deuteronomy sermon 34, 203-204.

Whereas the *Institutes* are the best source for Calvin's Sabbath theology, his Sabbath ethics are not developed there. In two Deuteronomy sermons, preached from the pulpit of St. Pierre in June 1555, he sets forth guidelines for practical Sabbath observance. These are sermons 34 and 35, Nicholas Bound's most frequent Calvin references.[10]

In sermon 34 Calvin develops the ethical implications of the first two of his three parts of the fourth commandment. He begins by stressing at length the typological, ceremonial character of the Sabbath. As a foreshadowing of spiritual, eternal rest, the Sabbath has been fulfilled by Christ and "now that the thing itself is given unto us, we must no more stay upon the shadows." Yet there remains an internal meaning. The Sabbath rest points to the truth that God's people must separate themselves from their sins. In the church today this separation or holy rest is found in Christ, but the ancient Israelites needed signs and symbols of their release from sin. For them the Sabbath was "a warrant of the grace that was purchased us to mortify our thoughts and affections, that God might live in us by the power of his holy spirit."

It is clear once again that Calvin's grace theology controls his view of the Sabbath. Keeping the Sabbath means most fundamentally to depart from the bondage of sin into the freedom of God's grace. In the new order ushered in by Christ, keeping the Sabbath means first of all a constant, daily resting from sinful deeds. Calvin declares that since Christ's coming "we be no more tied to the old bondage of keeping the Sabbath day." Yet, "in substance," the commandment must be observed by the suppression of human desire, will, and works, and by openness to the will and work of God. This is the rest required by the fourth commandment. "And how must we rest? We must stand at a stay, so as our thoughts run not roving abroad, to invent one thing or other." Whenever people are full of "envy, rancor, ambition, cruelty and guilt," they break the Sabbath commandment. But when they dedicate themselves to God and submit to the guidance and governance of his Spirit, then they faithfully observe the substance of the Sabbath command. The Sabbath, therefore, teaches "a perfect doctrine of holiness." Calvin calls the renunciation of self and total dedication to God the "spiritual keeping of the Sabbath of the Lord." He

---

[10]The citations that follow in this portion of the chapter, unless otherwise noted, are from the Golding translation, pp. 200-10.

repeats, "We be no more bound to the ceremony that was kept so straitly under the law."

Christians have much more liberty regarding the use of the particular day than did the Jews of old. It is a liberty "purchased for us by the death and passion of our Lord Jesus Christ." But that increased liberty does not mean diminished responsibility for Christians. The spiritual keeping of the Sabbath is not just for one day a week but for all time and eternity. In Calvin's words, "The rest that God commandeth us is everlasting, and not by pangs or fits as they say." From that perspective, the spiritual keeping of the Sabbath is far more demanding than the mere external observance of a day. Anyone can take external rest from labor, but only by the grace and spirit of God can people rest from their sinful works and allow God to work in them redemptively.

This first point of Calvin's Sabbath ethics flows clearly and directly from the first point of his three-dimensional Sabbath theology. Sabbath rest is essentially redemptive rest in Christ. For Christian life this implies the mortification of the old person of sin, and the putting on of the new person in Christ.

The second function of the fourth commandment is to provide a time for communal worship. Calvin says, "For that day was ordained for men to assemble in, to hear the doctrine of the law preached, to communicate together with sacrifices, and to call upon the name of God." In his elaboration of this second aspect of Sabbath keeping, Calvin sounds very much like the Sabbatarians. In fact, most of Bound's references are to this portion of sermon 34.

Calvin calls for a literal, physical cessation of daily labor on the Lord's Day, not as an end in itself, but to provide time for worship of God. Recreational activity should also be suspended, for such activity interferes with worship as certainly as daily labor does. "If we spend the Lord's day in making good cheer, and in playing and gaming," he writes, "is that a good honouring of God? Nay, is it not a mockery, yea and a very unhallowing of his name." Calvin urges that shop windows be shut on the Lord's Day, that travel be curtailed and recreation avoided so that there be sufficient time and freedom to hear from God's Word, to meet together and make confession of faith, to pray, and to use the sacraments. Calvin bemoans the neglect of worship in the Geneva of his day: "And though the bell toll to bring them to the sermon, yet it seems to them that they have nothing else to do but to think upon their business, and to cast up their accounts concerning this and that matter. Other some fall to gluttony, and shut themselves in their houses, because they dare not show a manifest contempt in the open streets."

Calvin takes an additional step in this second part of his Sabbath ethics. Like the English Sabbatarians, he argues that the Sabbath should be used not only for public worship and hearing sermons, but also that "we should apply the rest of the time to the praising of God." To use the Lord's Day to full advantage promotes that continued reflection on God's works that is required throughout the week. It will "fashion and polish" God's people for thanksgiving and praise "upon the Monday and all the week after." Conversely, if the people desecrate the Lord's Day, they are likely to "play the beasts all the week after." So they should not only publicly hear the sermon, but privately reflect on it. Calvin admonishes his Genevan congregation to "bend all [your] wits to consider the gracious things that God hath done for [you]," and to "dedicate that day wholly unto him so as we may be utterly withdrawn from the world." Even though the people of God in the present dispensation need not "keep the ceremony so straight as it was under the bondage of the law," it is nonetheless important to "consider how our Lord requireth to have this day bestowed in nothing else, but in hearing of his word, in making common prayer, in making confession of our faith, and in having the use of the Sacraments."

He concludes the sermon with a brief summary, calling the people to spiritual rest in Christ and to the observance of an outward order for the purpose of worship and reflection on the words, works, and gracious gifts of God. In his closing words, he exhorts, "Let us show all the week after that we have profited in the same."

The third part of Calvin's Sabbath ethics is developed in Deuteronomy sermon 35, which covers especially the part of the fourth commandment that reads: "Six days you shall labor, and do all your work; but the seventh day is a sabbath to the Lord your God; in it you shall not do any work, you, or your son, or your daughter, or your manservant, or your maidservant, or your ox or your ass, or any of your cattle, or the sojourner who is within your gates, that your manservant and your maidservant may rest as well as you."

Calvin first rejects the view that the clause "six days you shall labor" should be regarded as a divine command to work for six full days.

God has only included those words as a reminder that he has given his people plenty of time for their own affairs, so it is not unreasonable for him to require that one day out of seven be set aside for worship. Calvin alludes again to the totality of service on the Lord's Day and at one point speaks of God's requirement of "the seventh part of your time." It is, once again, clear from this passage that while Calvin was not absolutely committed to the one-in-seven rhythm, he does take it very seriously and considers it a normal and typical routine for the Christian community.

In the remainder of this sermon, Calvin elaborates on the social implications of the fourth commandment's requirement that rest be granted to servants and beasts of burden and "the stranger that is within thy gates." He clearly regards this requirement as applicable to the Christian community as well as to the ancient Jewish people. On the day of worship servants, strangers, and beasts of burden are to be given the opportunity for physical rest. But this rest is designed primarily for the benefit of God's people and only secondarily for the servants, strangers, and animals themselves. When beasts of burden are released from their labors on this day, they serve as a reminder to God's people of the need for rest. With the "stables and stalls shut up," there is a "monument before our eyes" calling for Sabbath observance. Calvin refers to the Sabbath as a sacrament twice in this context.

Nowhere in his view of the Sabbath does Calvin suggest that the Sabbath has anything to do with people's need for physical rest. He therefore has a bit of trouble with the requirement for servant rest. God's intention, says Calvin, was not to grant servants a day of rest "so as they should be tired." So the servant's rest is an "overplus" or an "accessory." It is a fringe benefit, not at the heart of the Sabbath's intent; the primary concern is the service of God and growth in holiness and obedience. And yet, Calvin says that the command to give servants rest has social, not spiritual purpose: "Here it should seem that God ordained not the Sabbath day for a spiritual order only, as is said afore, but also for charity's sake." This part of the commandment, therefore, should remind the "haves" to deal compassionately with the "have-nots," that is, with "the poor . . . all underlings and subjects, and of all such as (to our seeming) are not worthy to be compared or matched with us in respect of the world." In spite of differing social and economic stations in life, mankind is "knit together as one flesh."

All are created in the image of God. When I meet another, says Calvin, "There ought I to behold my self as in a looking glass." The Jews were also called upon to remember their once-desperate condition as slaves in Egypt. Reflecting on this, Calvin says that consideration of their own misery prompts God's people to discharge more readily their responsibilities toward others. Shared experiences with the oppressed leads to more charitable attitudes. He concludes this passage with an interesting comment about the golden rule as natural law. "We ought at leastwise to do to other folks as we ourselves would be done unto. Nature teaches us that, and we need not go to school to learn it."

With regard to "the stranger within thy gates," Calvin again urges that the benefits resulting from rest are primarily for God's people, not for strangers. These strangers are to rest lest God's people be led astray by evil example. For this reason (and apparently this reason only) Calvin defends legislation enforcing this commandment along with the others in the first table of the law. Laws against blasphemy are necessary because the God-despisers who blaspheme may lead Christians astray. Similarly, Sabbath rest must be enforced. Only in this sense is it a commandment for all people.

This survey of Calvin's Sabbath position reveals both significant differences and striking similarities between him and the English Sabbatarians. They differed most sharply in their respective theological interpretations of the Sabbath commandment. It is not at all surprising that the Sabbatarians never cited the *Institutes* for support, for it was there that Calvin's Sabbath theology was best summarized. Calvin and the Sabbatarians disagreed on the two cardinal principles of Sabbatarian theology. Bound gave clear expression to these principles when he argued that the Sabbath command is rooted in the Creation order and is therefore moral and universal in scope. In addition, he insisted that the first day of the week and no other is especially sanctified by God as the Sabbath, making it literally the Christian Sabbath.

Calvin did not express these views. He seems at times to flirt with the idea of some abiding, internal connection between the Sabbath and Creation, but he falls short of declaring the fourth commandment a Creation ordinance. He only uses God's rest after his creative activity as an alluring example for both Jews and Christians to follow. For Calvin the Sabbath is not, therefore, a universal, moral law binding on all humankind. Calvin, in fact, stresses the ceremonial, typological significance of the Jewish Sabbath much more than its moral significance. And, of course, his treatment places heavy emphasis on the abolition of this ceremonial meaning of the Sabbath and its fulfillment in Christ. Calvin's stress on the ceremonial nature of the commandment leads him to give persistent warnings against reverting to the old Jewish observance of days and clinging to shadow rites. The Sabbatarians not only failed to warn of this danger, they fell into it. Moreover, Calvin does not hold, as the Sabbatarians did, that the Christian community is absolutely tied to the observance of the first day of the week or even to the rhythm of one day in seven, except as a minimal requirement. He regards the first day of the week appropriate for worship because it is the day of Christ's Resurrection, but he rejects as a "superstitious observance of days" any attempt to turn the first day of the week into a Christian Sabbath directly akin to the Jewish Sabbath of the fourth commandment.

While the Sabbatarians stressed the morally binding principles of the fourth commandment and of the New Testament apostolic practice, Calvin, with a greater spirit of flexibility and freedom, emphasized the practical need for good order in the church. It is in the interest of good order that Christians today should make use of the pattern provided by the fourth commandment. This is literally *good* order for none other than God provided it for the ancient Israelites. Since the Christian community is no less in need of such order than were the Jews of old, Christians should continue to use the fourth commandment for ordering and providing time for both communal and private worship today. It should be emphasized again, however, that "good order" was a very high priority for Calvin. Consequently, one should never conclude from his stern warning against Sabbatarian superstition that Calvin wanted to abandon the traditional use of a weekly day of rest and worship. He urged the continued use of the fourth commandment "in order to prevent religion from either perishing or declining among us."

There are both differences and unmistakable similarities between Calvin and the Sabbatarians in their respective views of the ethical implications of the fourth commandment. The most significant difference appears in connection with Calvin's first of the three purposes of the Sabbath. Since the Sabbath represents spiritual, redemptive rest, keeping the Sabbath means departing from sinful works so God may work in us. The English Sabbatarians did not develop such a doctrine nor its subsequent ethic.

On the other hand, in his second reason for the Sabbath, Calvin and the Sabbatarians recommend remarkably similar uses of the Lord's Day. Both call for cessation of daily labor and recreation, not as an end in itself, but to provide opportunity for worship. Both assert that this worship should extend throughout the day and should involve private meditation as well as public assembly. With respect to the social ethic arising from the last part of the fourth commandment, there are also marked similarities between Calvin and the Sabbatarians.

In short, while Calvin was not Sabbatarian on the crucial theological issues, in practice he made certain recommendations quite similar to those of the authors of the English Sabbath treatises. At the same time, Calvin and the Sabbatarians differed in their overall approaches to Sabbath ethics. Calvin's approach was colored by his practical concern for good order in the church. The Sabbatarian approach, reflected in Bound and later in the Westminster Confession, was a more principled approach, basing the Christian observance of a day of rest and worship more directly and immediately on the law of the fourth commandment. Calvin, moreover, added an extremely important ethical dimension when he drew from the fourth commandment the sweeping, spiritual, redemptive conclusion that Christians are only keeping the Sabbath when they rest from their evil works and let God work in them by his Spirit all the days of their lives.

It is extremely important to note that on the most critical, definitive Sabbatarian issue—the divine appointment of Sunday as the New Testament, Christian Sabbath—Calvin was decidedly non-Sabbatarian. Anti-Sabbatarians like Peter Heylyn could, and did, draw on Calvin for support against the Sabbatarians on this point. The only legitimate claim the Sabbatarians could make to the prestigious backing of Calvin was in the practical area of Sabbath observance; for even on the matter of the creation origins of the fourth commandment, Calvin was ambiguous at best.

Much the same can be said about Bucer and Bullinger, the two Continental contemporaries of Calvin who exerted the most significant influence upon the English reformers. Martin Bucer, the Strasbourg reformer, though Regius Professor of Divinity at Cambridge for only two years (from 1549 until his death in 1551), commanded great respect in England. Indisputably, he left a deep imprint upon English Reformed thought and life.[11] Like Calvin, Bucer made statements about Sabbath observance that must have encouraged high Sabbath views. For example, he wrote concerning the first day of the week, the day "on which our dear Lord Christ rose from the dead," that "we should consecrate this day to God and celebrate it with spontaneous piety and no less zeal than was demanded of the ancients in their sanctification of the sabbath." Bucer appeals for support not only to 1 Corinthians 16:2 but also to Exodus 20:8-11, 31:12-17, and 35:1ff. After reciting the well-known public worship duties of the day, at the heart of which is "to hear the word of God read and preached," he adds, "and the whole day is to be spent in the pursuit of piety."[12] In discussing the examination of candidates for ordination, Bucer includes an appeal to interrogate each candidate about his view of the Lord's day. A candidate should be asked

> whether he believes that we incur God's stern displeasure when we fail to devote the Lord's Day and other specially consecrated days to godly exercises, abandoning not merely useful physical labours, but much more all the useless and harmful works of the flesh. . . . For whatever lawful recreations to the people are granted, it can never be rightly permitted on days especially set apart for divine worship. God has himself pronounced that anyone who violates such days should be cut off from among his people, and even be removed by bodily death from among all people.[13]

This was tough talk about the Sabbath, worthy of the most extreme Sabbatarians. Bucer, however, did not delve deeply into the theology of the Sabbath, and may be regarded as, at most, a practical Sabbatarian.

---

[11]Regarding Bucer, see August Lang, *Puritanismus und Pietismus* (Darmstadt: Wissenchaftlicke Buchgesellschaft, 1972) 13-38; Constantin Hopf, *Martin Bucer and the English Reformation* (Oxford: Basil Blackwell, 1946).

[12]*Commonplaces of Martin Bucer*, trans. and ed. D. F. Wright (Appleford: Sutton Courtenay, 1972) 90.

[13]Ibid., 264.

Henry Bullinger was another of the earlier reformers to whom English Sabbatarians appealed.[14] He was one of the more influential and widely read Continental theologians in England. The popularity of Bullinger's *Decades* is attested by their translation into English as early as 1577. In 1586 Archbishop Whitgift included among his "Orders for the Better Increase of Learning in the Inferior Ministers" a stipulation for weekly exposure to the *Decades*.[15]

Regarding the two central issues in Sabbatarian theology, the Sabbatarians had Bullinger's support for one, but not for the other. To wit, Bullinger does not emphasize the ceremonial character of the fourth commandment as heavily as Calvin. The commandment has a ceremonial dimension "so far forth as it is joined to sacrifices and other Jewish ceremonies, and so far forth as it is tied to a certain time," but the commandment is perpetual "in respect that on the sabbath-day religion and true godliness are exercised and published, that a just and seemly order is kept in the church, and the love of our neighbour is thereby preserved."[16]

Later in the *Decades*, in a sermon on "The Ceremonial Laws of God," Bullinger explicitly affirms the creation origin of the Sabbath.

> The sabbath was observed by a natural and divine law even from the first creation of the world, and is the chief of all other holy days. For it was not then first ordained by Moses, when the ten commandments were given by God from Heaven: for the keeping of the sabbath was received of the saints immediately from the beginning of the world. And therefore we read that the Lord in the commandments did say: "Remember that thou keep holy the sabbath-day." And before the law was given, there is evident mention made of the sabbath in the sixteenth of Exodus, and the second of Genesis.[17]

On the alteration issue, the Sabbatarians could make only selective use of Bullinger. Although the day has been changed to Sunday "be-

[14]Regarding Bullinger, see J. W. Baker, *Heinrich Bullinger and the Covenant: The Other Reformed Tradition* (Athens: Ohio University Press, 1980).

[15]Edward Cardwell, *Synodalia* (Oxford University Press, 1842) 2:562; John Strype, *John Whitgift* (Oxford: Clarendon Press, 1822) 3:194.

[16]Henry Bullinger, *Decades* (Cambridge: Parker Society, 1849) 1-2:259.

[17]Ibid., 3:162.

cause of the Lord's glorious resurrection upon that day," nevertheless "we do not in any part of the apostles' writings find any mention made that this Sunday was commanded us to be kept holy." At the same time, "it would be against all godliness and christian charity, if we should deny to sanctify the Sunday: especially, since the outward worship of God cannot consist without an appointed time and space of holy rest."[18]

Other motifs introduced by Bullinger became major themes in the Sabbatarian treatises: the significance of the word *remember*, the four main elements of public worship, the law of equity, and God's example as a reason for our Sabbath keeping.[19] The significance of the word *remember* is "that the sabbath was of old ordained, and given first of all to the ancient fathers, and then again renewed by the Lord, and beaten into the memory of the people of Israel." God's example in the Creation week is a supreme reason for Sabbath keeping today. It also is a reminder that on the Sabbath, "we must think of the works that God did in the six days." Furthermore, just as God's work of providential care did not cease on the seventh day, so too his people may perform good works on the Sabbath.

Bullinger incorporates a separate section on abuses of the Sabbath and outlines harsh punishment for Sabbath breakers.[20] Among the abuses of the Sabbath day, he mentions the "provoking of fleshly pleasures" such as dicing, drinking, and dancing. He also mentions an abuse that later reappears in Richard Greenham's Sabbath treatise. Bullinger declares that they who "lie wrapt in bed and fast asleep till the day be almost spent, not once thinking to make one of God's congregation," break the fourth commandment. Scriptural threats of severe punishment for Sabbath breakers should prompt serious Sabbath keeping today, according to Bullinger. It is the duty of magistrates to "compel to amendment the breakers and contemners of God's sabbath and worship." Then, in an astonishingly harsh statement, Bullinger suggests that it is appropriate to punish Sabbath breakers "by bodily imprisonment, by loss of goods, or by death." On the other hand, he is relatively permissive regarding necessary Sabbath labor, saying it is

---

[18]Ibid., 1-2:260.

[19]Ibid., 254-58.

[20]Ibid., 262-64.

lawful "on the sabbath to underset with props a ruinous house that is ready to fall" and "to gather in, and keep from spoiling, the hay or corn, which, by reason of unseasonable weather, hath lain too long abroad."[21]

This trio of early Continental reformers—Calvin, Bucer, and Bullinger—all of whom profoundly influenced English Reformed thought and practice, were agreed on the practical importance of a weekly day of worship. But Bullinger was the only one who contributed at all to Sabbatarian theology. All three believed that the fourth commandment had continuing relevance, obliging Christians to devote one day in seven to rest and worship. However, it was chiefly their strong position on Sabbath observance that provided support for later developments in England.

A more distinctive Sabbatarian motif does appear in the Continental Reformed tradition later in the century. This is best reflected in the writings of Francis Junius and Jerome Zanchius. Junius was born in Bourges in 1545. He received some of his theological training in Geneva and was a parish pastor in Antwerp for a time. Junius finished his professional life in the university, first teaching at Heidelberg and then at Leyden, where he died in 1602.[22] The Sabbatarian motif in his thought is most evident in his "Praelections on Genesis 2," a passage to which Bound often appeals in his Sabbath treatises.[23]

God's blessing and sanctification of the seventh day sets it apart from the other days in Junius's view: "Besides the common blessing which it had with the other days by the law of nature, it had a special blessing of holiness." The fourth commandment has its origin in Creation, for "God did then command it to be kept holy." He comments further on Genesis 2:3 saying, "There are two things to be observed in this text. First what God ordained on the seventh day, and then what was the cause of that ordinance. That which he ordained consists of two parts, one that God blessed the seventh day, the other that he

[21]Ibid., 265.

[22]Regarding Junius, see F. W. Cuno, *Franciscus Junius* (Amsterdam: von Scheffer and Co., 1891).

[23]Francis Junius, *Seu Creationis a Deo factae* (Heidelberg, 1589) 60ff.

sanctified it, and by the former he means that he appointed it to be a blessed day; by the other, that he commanded that this blessed day should be kept holy by man and be spent in holy exercises."[24]

Junius does not deny a ceremonial element in the fourth commandment. Nevertheless, he stresses its essentially moral character: "The substance of this law is natural and therefore is placed in the fourth precept of the decalogue as that which is to be observed of all men alike. That which is natural, namely that every seventh day should be kept holy unto the Lord, that still remains although that seventh day be changed. That which is positive, namely that day which was the seventh day from creation should be the sabbath, that is now changed in the Church of God."[25]

Of all the Continental Reformed theologians of his day, Junius was probably the most emphatically Sabbatarian on the vital issue of the change of day. He asserts that the change to the New Testament Sabbath came with the authority of Jesus Christ himself. "The cause of this change," he says, "is the resurrection of Christ, and the benefit of establishing the church in Christ; the commemoration of which benefit succeeded the memory of creation, not by human tradition, but by Christ's own observation and appointment, who both in the very day of his resurrection and every eighth day after, until his ascension appeared unto his disciples, and came into their assemblies, and the same is still kept of the Church of God, unto which the apostles have delivered the observation of the Lord's day by the appointment and example of Christ."[26]

Commenting directly on the issue that would eventually become the center of the English controversy, Junius declares: "Therefore, since the Lord's day by Christ's action, example, and institution, by the constant observation of the apostles and the ancient church, and by the testimony of the Scripture has been observed and put in the place of the Jewish sabbath; they are absurd who declare that the observation of the Lord's day continues in the church by tradition, and not by the authority of Holy Scripture."[27]

[24]Ibid., 61.

[25]Ibid., 63.

[26]Ibid.

[27]Ibid., 64.

Jerome Zanchius, the Italian-born, Heidelberg theologian, was highly regarded in England. The English translator of his *Speculum Christianum* extols his writings in terms appropriate to Holy Writ. "They are exceeding effectual, " he says, "befitting this sinful and sottish age. . . . They are fruitful in many considerations; to prevent curiosity; to abandon security; to rouse up the drowsy Christian; to detect the temporizers; to kindle zeal; to work vigilance; to enforce repentance; to minister consolation; to teach the wise; to hearten the weak; to confirm faith and hope of heaven and happiness."[28] Considering these accolades, it is not surprising that in the Sabbatarian disputes of the early seventeenth century, no one is quoted more frequently than Zanchius. As noted above, there is not a single reference to him in Nicholas Bound's 1595 *Treatise of the Sabbath*, but in the expanded 1606 edition Zanchius quotations exceed all others. Other early Sabbatarians, especially Perkins, were acquainted with the works of Zanchius.[29] While Perkins does not appeal explicitly to Zanchius in his treatment of the fourth commandment, there are similarities between the two approaches both in form and content.

The overall structure of Zanchius's thought is, in fact, very similar to that of Perkins. A key figure in the development of Reformed Scholasticism, Zanchius gives predestination a prominent and controlling position in his theology. But like so many of the late-sixteenth-century Reformed theologians, there is a strong ethical accent in his thought as well. He emphasizes heavily the role of the good life patterned after the law of God and providing confirmation of election.

Therefore, the law receives great emphasis. Zanchius ascribes a power and function to the Decalogue that one might expect to be applied to Christ himself. The Decalogue is a "true and lively picture of the image of God," he writes, for it shows us "what man was in his first estate, and what he was made in his second estate, and what man-

---

[28]Jerome Zanchius, *Speculum Christianum* (London, 1614), Epistle Dedicatory. Regarding Zanchius, see Otto Gründler, *Die Gotteslehre Girolami Zanchis und ihre Bedeutung für seine Lehre von der Prädestination* (Neukirchener Verlag der Enziehungsverein, 1965).

[29]Perkins includes a translation of a portion of a Zanchius treatise at the end of his famous *Case of Conscience, the Greatest That Ever Was* (London: J. Legat, 1595).

ner of one he ought to be; and further what he should afterwards be in the third estate in part, and what perfectly in the fourth." So the law teaches "what we were, what we are, what we ought to be, and indeed what we shall be, if we trust in Christ."[30]

In his discussion of the Decalogue, Zanchius devotes an astonishing 200 pages to the fourth commandment, a strong signal of his Sabbatarian leanings.[31] He includes in this treatment many aspects of ecclesiology—for example, church, ministry, and sacraments. Zanchius is probably unique among the reformers in his use of the fourth commandment as the biblical-theological gateway to ecclesiology.

The fourth commandment has both moral and ceremonial dimensions according to Zanchius. It is moral, he says, "in that nature teaches and piety binds us, that some one day be appointed as a rest from servile works, that the church may more freely give itself to the worship of God. It is ceremonial, and peculiarly pertains to the Jews, in so far as the seventh day is prescribed and no other." He is emphatic about the Creation origin of the commandment. The word *remember* is used,

> for by it God would signify that this precept to sanctify the sabbath day was not then first prescribed by him unto the people: for it was delivered from the beginning of the world unto Adam and to the rest of the fathers in remembrance that the world was created in six days, and of that rest which God himself kept on the seventh day. And therefore it is not simply said, sanctify the sabbath, but *remember* to sanctify it, so that this word looks both forward and backward, backward because it shows that this day was dedicated to the worship of God from the creation of the world, forward because it admonishes us that we should never forget it.[32]

Zanchius believes New Testament worship is directly regulated by the fourth commandment. "It is to be observed, that it is not said, 'Remember thou keep holy the seventh day,' but 'the Sabbath day,' the day of rest." This makes the fourth commandment more immediately applicable to the New Testament situation. God "did not sanctify the

---

[30]Jerome Zanchius, *A Brief Discourse, Taken Out of the Writings of Her. Zanchius* (London, 1595) 48.

[31]Jerome Zanchius, *Operum Theologicorum* (N.p., 1605) 2:648-856.

[32]Ibid., 653.

seventh day precisely, . . . but the day consecrated unto rest," regard-
less of whether that is the seventh or the first. Although the day of rest
was originally the seventh day, "after the coming of Christ he would
not have us tied to sanctify this day. . . . but only that we should keep
that day which by the apostles was dedicated to holy rest and was allowed of all the churches, and this is the Lord's day. And for this cause
the Lord in the substance of the commandment did not put the seventh day, but the sabbath day."[33]

On the critical alteration issue Zanchius regards the first day of the
week as the Christian Sabbath since the Resurrection of Christ. He admits that "we have no express command from the apostles to sanctify
the Lord's day; yet we doubt not that it is an apostolic tradition." After
gathering lengthy supporting evidence from the early church fathers,
he adds, "It is not ineptly gathered out of Holy Scripture that the sub-
stitution of the Lord's day in place of the seventh proceeds from the
apostles." And in another place he writes, "Therefore this day is the
first and chief holy day that the Church of Christ has always kept."[34]

With regard to Sabbath observance, Zanchius emphasizes rest from
"servile labour" and even develops a small catalog of prohibitions. The
ordinary labors of one's livelihood are to be set aside on the Sabbath
"because they are impediments and hindrances to men, that they cannot attend upon those things, which God requires in his outward worship." Such things are to be avoided as "to use merchandise, to open
the shopwindows, to sell, to buy, and such like things in the city; and
at home to spin, to sew, to weave, to wash, to dress up houses" and
other things that "belong unto the profit and commodity of this life."
He strongly emphasizes the householder's responsibility to enable his
entire household to worship, argues that the cattle must rest so they
will not be a means of drawing people away from the worship of God,
and urges the legislation of the Sabbath by magistrates.

But the best from Zanchius is a breathtakingly speculative theological flight of fancy in which he muses upon the meaning of Genesis 2:3
in "De Hominis Creatio." Here is Continental Sabbatarianism at its
best—or at least at its most creative. It is such an extraordinary inter-

[33]Ibid., 657.

[34]Ibid., 669-74.

pretation that the passage is included here in its entirety. This is Zanchius's understanding of how God blessed and sanctified the seventh day.

> For seeing that he did rest himself upon the seventh day from the work of creation, and nothing more remained to be done, therefore he wanted this seventh day, by resting from other works, to be consecrated to work of another kind. And what else could that be but that he declared unto Adam and Eve all things that he had done and to what end he had created them and what happiness was prepared for them in heaven; how they ought to worship him and other things which appertained both to their duties and their everlasting happiness? I doubt not, therefore (I will tell you mine opinion, without the prejudice of others), I doubt not, I say, but that the Son of God, taking upon himself the shape of man, was occupied that whole seventh day in most holy colloquies with Adam, and that he did also fully make himself known to Adam and Eve, and revealed the manner and order which he had used in creating all things, and exhorted them both to meditate upon those works, and in them to acknowledge their creator and to praise him. And that by his own example he admonished them to occupy themselves especially in this exercise of godliness setting all other business aside; and also that they would so instruct and teach their children. To be short, I doubt not but that in that seventh day he taught them all divinity; and held them occupied in hearing him, and in praising and giving thanks to God their Creator for so many and great benefits. And I am led to this interpretation of the text by these two reasons: whereof the first is taken from the sanctification of the sabbath which God prescribed in the law, and that is, that men then forsaking all worldly business should give themselves to the contemplation of the work and benefits of God, and to the knowledge and praising and worshipping of God. And also that they, neglecting the affections and works of their own flesh should suffer God to work in them by his holy spirit; therefore such was the sanctification of the seventh day (as concerning mankind) of which Moses speaks here. Another reason is, because that Adam ought to understand the sanctification of such a day; therefore it is probable that the Son of God opened this unto Adam and Eve both in plain words, and also by his own example. For even God also is said to rest upon that day, and in Exodus he exhorts the sanctification of the sabbath by his own example; therefore he sanctified it with Adam and Eve. This is my opinion of the sanctification of the seventh day, in which God rested from all his work that he had made, namely that Christ spent that whole day in instructing our first parents, and in exercising them in the worship of God, and

in admonishing them, that they should teach the same things to their posterity.[35]

Nicholas Bound was enamored of this passage, quoting from it extensively in support of the Creation origins of the Sabbath and of the fourth commandment.[36] The large number of Zanchius citations in Bound's work, *Sabbathum Veteris*, attest to the importance of this Continental Reformed Scholastic for the development of Sabbatarianism in England.

The most important contribution made by the Continental Reformed tradition to the development of Sabbatarianism in England was described in the preceding chapter: it provided the matrix, the context, the theological environment in which the sanctified life became a matter of critical importance and God's revealed will for that life a matter of passionate concern. This concern led theologians and pastors to renewed study of the Decalogue and especially to the precept in the law that speaks of the need for a sacred time devoted exclusively to the development and cultivation of the life of the spirit. Earlier Continental reformers such as Calvin, Bucer, and Bullinger recognized the continuing need for such holy time, but fell short of calling for a New Testament Sabbath. Fourth commandment interpretations of later Continental Reformed theologians such as Junius and Zanchius, however, edged closer to genuine Sabbatarianism and could be used more legitimately to aid and abet the movement in late-sixteenth-century England.

And yet, because of differing historical circumstances, the Sabbath became an issue with much greater visibility in the English church than it ever received on the Continent. English church leaders wrote much more about the Sabbath than their Continental counterparts and became more preoccupied with precise rules about how to observe the Sabbath than was generally true on the Continent. They honed Sabbatarian theology with greater care and precision and brought it to new levels of sophistication. It is, therefore, more accurate to conclude that the English Sabbatarians looked to the Continent for the confirmation

---

[35]Ibid., 1:538, 539.

[36]Bound, *Sabbathum Veteris*, 19, 20.

of their views rather than to claim that the origin of those views is to be found on the Continent. One can search fervently among the Continental reformers for that elusive origin of Sabbatarianism, only to realize anew that Sabbatarianism remains largely an English contribution to Reformed theology.

7

SABBATARIANISM AND
PURITAN THEOLOGY

PERHAPS SABBATARIANISM was not entirely a new creation wrought by the Puritans, but it is indisputable that the Sabbath, both in England and New England, eventually became the heartbeat of Puritan Christianity. It is not surprising, therefore, to discover within the Sabbatarian treatises certain theological themes fundamental to all of Puritan thought and life. When Sabbatarianism and Puritanism are too sharply distinguished, as they are in Kenneth Parker's work, we are deprived of an important and convenient lens through which to view these Puritan fundamentals.

There have been many attempts to analyze and isolate the main features of English Puritan thought, but none of them approaches that task through the Sabbath.[1] And yet, an issue of such momentous concern to the Puritans is certain to divulge some of the best clues to the basic elements of their faith and life.

---

[1]See, for example, John S. Coolidge, *The Pauline Renaissance in England* (London: Clarendon, 1970); Charles George and Katherine George, *The Protestant Mind of the English Reformation* (Princeton: Princeton University Press, 1961); Patrick McGrath, *Papists and Puritans* (London: Blandford, 1967). Herbert Richardson uses the Sabbath as the clue to the basic creational motif in Puritan theology (*Toward an American Theology* [New York: Harper & Row, 1967] ch. 5).

Three biblical theological motifs functioned powerfully in English Sabbatarianism: the motifs of Creation, Resurrection, and sanctification. It was essentially these motifs, respectively, that provided the answers, to the three most hotly disputed aspects of Sabbatarianism: the institution, alteration, and celebration of the Sabbath. Vigorous debates between Sabbatarians and anti-Sabbatarians developed in these three areas by the end of the sixteenth century, becoming more heated and intense during the first half of the seventeenth.

One of the favorite topics for debate involved the scholastic distinction between moral and ceremonial law. Was the fourth commandment moral, ceremonial, or a little bit of both? This led, in turn, to the critical question about when the Sabbath was instituted. Was it a creative or redemptive ordinance? Is the fourth commandment rooted in Creation and hence a moral law applicable to all humankind for all time? Or is it part of the redemptive order for Israel, arising out of the Exodus and, therefore, simply one of the Old Testament typological ceremonies that have been fulfilled in Jesus Christ? The Sabbatarian position is clear: the fourth commandment is prelapsarian, etched indelibly on the human heart at Creation just as all the other moral laws were, observed by the patriarchs before the time of Moses, and simply reiterated or given written form at Sinai because of the sinfulness and weakness of humankind. An even more extreme position, forged in the passion of debate, was that the Sabbath commandment was explicitly communicated by God to Adam in paradise, thereby giving it a position of special prominence in the moral law. Nicholas Bound, appealing to Zanchius, declared that the Sabbath command "was first delivered by lively voice, namely to Adam and Eve in Paradise."[2] And Perkins argued that the Sabbath commandment was one of two commandments given by the Lord to Adam and Eve in the Garden of Eden.[3]

This Creation motif appears constantly in Sabbatarian literature. It is reflected in the opening words of every treatise, for each begins with a quotation of the fourth commandment from Exodus 20, with its familiar reference to God's example of work and rest in the creation of

---

[2]Bound, *Sabbathum Veteris*, 11.

[3]Perkins, *A Golden Chaine*, 20.

the world. The redemptive emphasis of Deuteronomy 5, where the Sabbath is tied to the deliverance out of Egypt, is sometimes mentioned in the course of the argument. But typically it is dismissed as a "secondary end" of the commandment, or as a temporary element relevant only to the Jews since the exodus-redemption was merely a shadowy type fulfilled by the coming of the cosmic redeemer, Jesus Christ. For the Sabbatarian, the central significance of the Sabbath is not to be found in the exodus from Egypt, but in the creation of the world. Sabbatarian thought was Creation-centered. Theologically, this was the nerve center of Sabbatarianism.

The Creation emphasis of Sabbatarianism has a variety of theological implications. Related to it, for example, is the Puritan emphasis on God as sovereign lawgiver and man as obedient lawkeeper. In Puritan thought, dominated as it was by ethical concern, the emphasis on God as lawgiver was very strong. The created order is a splendid structure of "natural law" designed by the divine architect. Humankind's basic responsibility is to live obediently within that structure. The Sabbath command demonstrates uniquely that this obedience is no mere legalism, for to observe the Sabbath is not only to live within God's law, but it is to share in the very life of God himself. The Sabbatarian emphasis is on God's example as the most important motive for human obedience. The Sabbath is a God-ordained law of the created order that God clearly observes, for he worked and rested according to the six-one rhythm at the time of creation. By keeping the Sabbath, God's people fit into the divine order for life in the created world.

The means God uses to govern and regulate life in the world is also related to this Creation theme. Much has been made of the Puritan emphasis on Scripture as the supreme and sole authority. In a fallen world, the Scriptures communicate the divine will and plan for humankind. But in Puritanism there is also a persistent appeal to a natural law that is not in conflict with Scripture but surely antedates it, for it is given in and with Creation. Sabbatarian treatises make frequent reference to natural law. Part of that natural law embedded in Creation is the moral law summarized in the Ten Commandments. These laws, including the fourth commandment, like all natural laws of creation, are perpetual and binding on all people for all time. Peter Barker writes, for example, that "in the first age of the world from Adam to Moses, men had no other guide to conduct them for the carriage of their lives, than the law of nature; which S. Paul calleth a law written on the heart, and others, *Jus gentium,* the law of nations."[4]

George Walker calls the law of the Sabbath a natural law in yet another sense when he describes it as "that which the very light of natural reason shows to be most convenient and necessary for men now corrupt, and which so soon as it is commanded and revealed by God's word appears so necessary in the very nature of it, both for men's souls and bodies, that without it they cannot have ordinarily any well-being on earth, nor escape hell and come to heaven after death."[5]

The Puritans had tremendous respect for the created order, a respect reflected in their attitude toward traditional patterns of earthly authority. Much has been made of the revolutionary impulse in Puritanism, but in the broadest and most representative stream of late-sixteenth-century Puritanism there were powerful conservative checks on that revolutionary potential. Though there is plenty of evidence that a Puritan with a Bible in his hand could be a powerful catalyst for change in society, there was also a broad stream of moderate Puritanism that had a deep respect for traditional sources of social control.[6] In Sabbatarian literature, at least until the 1630s, there is virtually no hint of a rebellious thought against the monarch, or even against the episcopal structure of the church. On the contrary, there are frequent declarations of devotion and loyalty, and regular appeals not only to heads of families but also to magistrates to ensure strict Sabbath keeping within their areas of authority. Sabbatarians considered the phrase "within thy gates" in the fourth commandment to be a reference to all areas of legal jurisdiction.

The Sabbatarian respect for six days of labor is also related to the Creation emphasis. In the treatises there is frequent appeal to the "law of equity," according to which God requires but one-seventh of the week's time and generously gives to his human subjects the other six-

⁴Peter Barker, *A Learned and Familiar Exposition upon the Ten Commandements* (London, 1633) fol. Bl.

⁵George Walker, *The Doctrine of the Holy Weekly Sabbath* (London, 1641) 78,79.

⁶Peter Lake, *Moderate Puritans and the Elizabethan Church* (Cambridge: at the University Press, 1982) 30ff. Cf. A. F. Scott Pearson, *Church and State* (Cambridge: at the University Press, 1928) ch. 4.

sevenths. But this does not mean that the activities of the six days are simply a matter of human prerogative. Rather, they are under the control of the Creator, whose six days of creative labor grace all human work. The Creator calls humankind to labor as well, and the six days are to be devoted to "ordinary vocations."[7] Richard Greenham links his concern for the six days of labor to the dispute about the moral or ceremonial character of the fourth commandment. He fears that if the commandment is ceremonial and therefore only for the ancient Jews, the reference to the six days of labor would also have to be regarded as irrelevant to the sixteenth century.[8]

In fact, the Puritan argument against the retention of the medieval Catholic holy days in the Church of England was based in part on this view of the vocational purpose of the six days. Sabbatarian treatises do not always sound culture-affirming; but in this context they surely are, since the six days of human labor are to be patterned after God's work in Creation. "The laboring hand," writes Peter Barker, "is the staple of the land, and raiseth up the pillars of it, without which the cords of the commonwealth would soon be loosed; for our good therefore God hath given us six days to labour, that by taking pain in them, we might live by the sweet of our own sweat."[9] Sabbatarians took special pains to distinguish the six days of labor from the one day of rest and worship because they were very sensitive to England's version of Anabaptism in the form of the "Family of Love," a group claiming that every day was a Sabbath for the Christian. Sabbatarians were not enticed by this pious-sounding belief. They feared that such a view would result in disorderliness and a neglect of regularly scheduled worship. As Thomas Fuller later put it, "These transcendents, accounting themselves mounted above the predicament of common piety, aver they need not keep any, because they keep all, days Lord's days, in their

---

[7]Perkins defines "vocation" as "a certain kind of life, ordained and imposed on man by God, for the common good" (*Workes*, 1:750). Cf. George and George, *Protestant Mind*, 126ff.

[8]Richard Greenham, *Works* (1612) 135.

[9]Barker, *Learned and Familiar Exposition*, 240.

elevated holiness. But alas! Christian duties, said to be over done, will prove never done, if not sometimes solemnly done."[10]

Because of its emphasis on holy rest and on spiritual activity such as prayer and meditation, Sabbatarian literature has a strong pietistic, devotional flavor. And yet, the Creation orientation kept the Sabbath rooted in this world. The Sabbath was not lifted out of daily life, but was part of the cosmic pattern and rhythm of life. As we have seen, there was respect for the six days as well as for the one. Moreover, Sabbatarians taught that Sabbath meditation was not simply to be introspective or otherworldly, but should be meditation "upon God's works," including the works of Creation. Richard Greenham ascribed a sacramental function to nature.

> Now as with the exercise of the word we have the sacraments to strengthen our faith; so with the meditating of the works of God we are to strengthen ourselves with the beholding of God his creatures, as the heavens and the scope, beauty, and continual course thereof, and the earth, which should have been all as pleasant as the garden of Eden, if Adam had continued in his innocency, whose work as it was by the light of nature to view the creatures of God, so also is it our work by the light of God's spirit.[11]

The Sabbath was to be used in part as a means to a deeper and fuller appreciation of this created world. While Sabbatarians generally did not emphasize or articulate the precise relationship between worship and work in God's world, such a relationship was assumed. Greenham mentions in passing that "as our callings serveth to God's worship, so God's worship sanctifieth our callings."[12]

The Resurrection did not figure in Sabbatarian thought as pervasively as the doctrines of Creation and sanctification. Nevertheless, it functioned significantly in what became an extremely important issue

---

[10]Fuller, *Church History*, 3:426. The same concern may help to explain why the eschatological interpretation of the Sabbath is almost totally absent in English Sabbatarian literature.

[11]Greenham, *Works*, 363. Bound also insists that meditation and conference on general revelation is required on the Sabbath (*Doctrine of the Sabbath*, 222).

[12]Greenham, *Works*, 373.

in the discussions and debates about the Sabbath: the issue of the alteration. The Sunday Sabbath became problematic for the Sabbatarians because of their heavy stress on a Sabbath controlled directly by the fourth commandment. The fourth commandment, after all, explicitly designates a certain day for worship, and it obviously is not the first day of the week. Yet one of the marks of English Sabbatarianism was its insistence that Sunday, and no other day, is the Christian's Sabbath. In every Sabbatarian treatise without exception, the key to the argument concerning the change of the day is the Resurrection of Jesus Christ.

While controversy in the area of institution remained fairly cool and restrained, debates about the alteration of the Sabbath day became heated and passionate. An especially sensitive issue between Sabbatarians and the Establishment was at stake: the issue of the scope of the church's authority. The Sabbatarians insisted that the alteration of the day of worship from the seventh to the first day of the week had biblical authority. By reason of Christ's Resurrection and in memory of that great event, the apostles altered the day of worship to the first day of the week. The Sabbath, therefore, stood apart from and above all the other holy days established by the church. Moreover, the Sabbatarians contended that it was not within the power of the church to change the day of worship. The anti-Sabbatarians responded that the establishment of a day of worship was essentially a pragmatic matter that must be left within the jurisdiction of earthly ecclesiastical decision makers. This became the major issue in the Sabbath disputes, and the challenge to the church's authority was the foremost cause of the sharp anti-Sabbatarian reaction from the ecclesiastical hierarchy at the turn of the century.[13]

In the debate about the alteration, however, the Sabbatarians never suggested an overhaul of the ecclesiastical power structure. They only insisted that the Sunday Sabbath rested upon the authority of Scripture itself. The first day of the week was the climax and end of the Lord's work, the day all Jewish ceremonies were fulfilled, so that "Christ himself brought in this change, and was the author of this day."[14] Many

---

[13]See above, ch. 4.

[14]Bound, *The Doctrine of the Sabbath*, 44.

other great events had occurred on the first day of the week: it was the first day of the creation of the world, the first day of the manna distribution in the wilderness, the day of Jesus' baptism, the day the 5,000 were fed, and the day of Pentecost. But none of these could compare with the greatest event of all: it was the day of Christ's Resurrection, an event of cosmic proportions. The first day of the week was the day "in which Christ Jesus the Creator of the new world, rested from his work of the new creation."[15]

It is common in Sabbatarian literature to find the appeal to the Resurrection leading to a discussion of the relative merits of redemption versus Creation. Perkins, for example, typically observes that the change of day was triggered by the Resurrection, declaring that "Christ in his own person gave them an example to celebrate and keep that day wherein he rose again for a Sabbath of the New Testament." He argues that one of the causes for the change was to provide "a more fit time for the memory of the work of man's redemption."[16] Redemption brings about a new creation, says Perkins, but he goes on to set redemption and the original work of Creation in a competitive framework.

> Nay this redemption is a more glorious work than the creation; for in that creation Adam was the head, but in this redemption Christ Jesus is our head. By the first creation we received a temporal life; but by redemption we received life eternal. In the creation Adam was espoused to Eve, but in the work of redemption every christian is espoused to Christ Jesus. By creation Adam had an earthly paradise: In this redemption we have an heavenly kingdom. In the creation God's power and wisdom did principally appear. In this redemption with power and wisdom he showed mercy and justice. . . . By creation he made man of nothing, but by redemption he made him of worse than nothing, and better than he was.[17]

The theology in Peter Barker's comparison is equally creative, but even more tenuous:

> Great was the work of creation, and therefore we must now mount upwards with the wings of nature; greater was the work of redemption,

---

[15]Ibid., 45, 46.

[16]Perkins, *A Godly and Learned Exposition or Commentarie upon the Three First Chapters of the Revelation* (London, 1606) 43.

[17]Ibid., 43, 44.

and therefore we must now soar aloft with the wings of grace. It cost more to redeem us than make us, for in our creation . . . he spake the words and it was done, but in our redemption, he spake, and did, and suffered many things; the one was the work of his fingers, the other the work of his arm. . . . He created the world in six days, but in restoring man he labored more than thirty years; in creating us, he gave us ourselves, in redeeming us, he gave himself for us; so that how much he is greater than we: so much is this day greater than that, and more worthily to be observed in regard to redeeming, than that in remembrance of creation, not now to be altered any more.[18]

Such interpretations may be fanciful, but they do serve to capture the buoyant tone of much of the Sabbatarian literature. One of the obstinate myths about the Puritan Sabbath is that it was a day of gloom and sadness rather than a day of gladness. Perhaps the legalism that soon entered into Sabbath keeping led to that point of view. The early Sabbatarian treatises, however, are consistently full of praise and hope, reflecting the mood of the Resurrection. The Sabbath is always viewed as a day of blessedness and quiet joy. Perhaps this is due, at least in part, to the fact that Sabbatarian thought is not dominated by the theology of the cross but by the open tomb. The cross, in fact, is conspicuously absent in Sabbatarian treatises. It is almost never mentioned and is obscured in any references to redemption by the doctrines of the Resurrection and sanctification.[19]

This set the Sabbath in a very positive framework. One of Richard Greenham's questions in his Sabbath-evening inventory was this: "Hath the Sabbath been our delight?"[20] And his answer to a question about Sunday weddings is revealing. He responds, "If it be demanded, whether this day be fit for marriage or no: I answer, it is, because on that day of rejoicing, there is a more lawful liberty of speech, and a more liberal use of cheerful behaviour." He nevertheless rec-

---

[18]Barker, *Learned and Familiar Exposition*, 243.

[19]Andreas Karlstadt's Sabbatarianism differs from English Sabbatarianism in this regard. Gordon Rupp points out that Karlstadt, the somewhat radical colleague of Luther and probably the first Protestant Sabbatarian, developed a theology of the Sabbath that is dominated by the cross. Karlstadt viewed the day as one of gloom and sadness. G. Rupp, *Patterns of Reformation* (London: Epworth, 1969) 130.

[20]Greenham, *Works*, 368.

ommends that wedding feasts be held on another day, primarily because they create a demand for labor that ill befits the Sabbath rest.[21]

The various questions concerning the celebration or observance of the Sabbath aroused emotions, for such questions could not remain on the level of the theoretical and abstract. They touched people's lives in sensitive and visible places, for a strict observance of the Sabbath rest had obvious social and economic implications. In fact, one cannot fully appreciate the meaning and significance of Sabbatarianism without an understanding of its fundamentally practical, pastoral nature. The heart and soul of the Sabbatarian movement is cut out if it is reduced to doctrinal and political questions about institution and alteration. Sabbatarianism was a way of life. The Sabbath, for the Puritan, was the chief means of sanctification.

As we have seen, the ideal of the sanctified life became a preoccupation of the Puritan mind of the late sixteenth century. Sabbatarianism developed in the context of the quest for personal holiness and for a holier church and commonwealth. This quest led to renewed interest in the Decalogue, especially in that one commandment of the ten that explicitly mentions holiness. The English Sabbatarians must have thought it ironic that this fourth commandment—regarded by them as the most indispensable—was precisely the commandment threatened with extinction because of ceremonial interpretation.

Every Sabbatarian treatise makes reference early on to God's sanctification of the Sabbath at the time of Creation and to humankind's obligation to "keep it holy" as well. Actually, sanctification in the fourth commandment was three-dimensional for the Sabbatarians: God sanctified the Sabbath day; his people must sanctify the Sabbath day; and through divine and human sanctification of the day, the Holy Spirit sanctifies humankind. In each of these dimensions, the idea of separation is important for understanding the meaning of sanctification. In sanctifying the Sabbath, God set it apart from the other days, designating it for rest and worship. Greenham expressed it as follows: "He sanctified, that is, put a part of the seventh day to his own worship, and blessed it with a peculiar blessing given to his worship ap-

[21]Ibid., 382.

pointed." This does not make the Sabbath inherently superior to the other days of the week. Regarding this point, Sabbatarians frequently appealed to the analogy of the sacramental elements. The bread and wine, though set apart for special use, are not per se superior; similarly, the seventh day is not superior to the other days, but is simply set apart or sanctified for worship. Only in this sense did God make a "special blessing above the other days, unto this day."[22]

God set the day apart for human use, and at this point the second and third dimensions become significant. Lancelot Andrewes writes, "God hath put apart this day, to the end that it might be applied wholly either to the means of sanctification, or to the practice of his sanctification begotten in us."[23] As God sanctified it with his blessing, so his creatures must sanctify the Sabbath with their obedience. Sanctification is the control word both in the Sabbatarians' view of the day and in their use of it. The Sabbath must be regarded as "holy to God," so that "behaviour be sanctified, tending to the practice of holiness."[24]

The Sabbath rest, therefore, is never an end in itself, but a means to the end of sanctification. In this light the Sabbatarians interpreted Mark 2:27 as follows: "The sabbath was made for man, not man for the sabbath." This means humans were not made for the Sabbath's rest, but for sanctification; "sanctification was his end, and man was made for it." Viewing this statement in light of the Sabbatarian insistence that even Adam "in his innocency" needed the Sabbath "for spiritual use and consideration"[25] makes it clear that sanctification did not simply mean personal cleansing from sin. Sabbatarians did not restrict sanctification to the redemptive sphere; they believed that it was applicable even to Creation. The Sabbatarians do not elaborate this idea, but it is implicit in their writings.

With regard to humanity's sanctification through the Sabbath, Bound sums up the Sabbatarian position nicely: "Therefore to conclude, I do most willingly acknowledge, that this was one principal end, for which the Sabbath was ordained: even that thereby we might be

---

[22]Ibid., 317.

[23]Andrewes, *Moral Law Expounded*, 327.

[24]Ibid., 328.

[25]Ibid., 328, 329.

sanctified through the pure use of God's worship upon that day; and that this should be the fruit of our resting, and sanctification of the day; without the which all that we do is to no purpose."[26] All of life, therefore, finds meaning and purpose in the Sabbath. Alluding to Exodus 31:17, Andrewes ascribes a sacramental function to the Sabbath when he says, "The Sabbath was a sign betwixt God and us; whereby we may know that it is he that sanctified us."[27]

The Sabbath is sanctified when it is properly observed. The central Sabbatarian emphasis regarding the observance of the Sabbath is the cessation of work throughout the entire day in order to enable attendance at public worship as well as to provide time for personal and family devotional life. It is particularly significant here that the conventional units of society are used in the sanctification process. The Holy Spirit is indeed the primary author of sanctification, but he uses the means of churches and families, and even the state.

Sabbath sanctification was to be achieved primarily, if not totally, in the context of corporate Christian experience. Every Sabbatarian treatise makes public worship the heart of Sabbath celebration. Gardiner's comment that "the Puritan could do all that was necessary for the observance of the day without crossing his own threshold" is dead wrong.[28] Peter Barker, for example, lashes out at private Sabbath keeping: "What a pride and niceness is it to turn church service only into parlor-praying and private preaching, when public service is in hand."[29]

The home, indeed, runs a close second to the church in its importance as a locale for Christian nurture on the Sabbath. One of the essential features of Puritanism is "the godly home ranged under the head

[26]Bound, *Sabbathum Veteris*, 47.

[27]Andrewes, *Moral Law Expounded*, 344, 345.

[28]Fuller, *History of England*, 3:247.

[29]Barker, *Learned and Familiar Exposition*, 230. John S. Coolidge argues against the traditional interpretation of Puritanism as heavily individualistic. Puritanism, he writes, "originates, then, in concern for the communal aspect of Christian experience." Puritans "expected faith to come to them normally by the hearing of the word in church. . . . The ceaseless nurture and growth of faith within the church is their incessant theme" (*Pauline Renaissance*, 147).

of the household for devotion and prayer."[30] Perkins calls the family a "little church" in his *Christian Oeconomie*, a treatise devoted to home and family. He writes, "Those families wherein this service of God is performed, are, as it were, little churches, yea even a kind of paradise upon earth."[31] William Gouge regards the family as the foundation of both the church and the commonwealth in the following statement:

> Oh if the head and several members of a family would be persuaded every one of them to be conscionable in performing their own particular duties, what a sweet society, and happy harmony would there be in houses? What excellent seminaries would families be to church and commonwealth? Necessary it is, that good order be first set in families; for as they were before other polities, so they are somewhat the more necessary; and good members of a family are like to make good members of church and commonwealth.[32]

The heads of households, therefore, were to play a key role in the sanctification of the Sabbath. "For this very cause," writes Perkins, "the fourth commandment is given first of all and principally to the master of the family, that he might see the sabbath kept and be a principal doer in all parts of God's worship therein."[33] Every Sabbatarian treatise includes a passage on the responsibility of the heads of households to administer a proper Sabbath for all "within their gates." The sanctification of English society into a godly commonwealth depended upon such traditional and familiar instruments of social control. In the Puritan scheme of things, reformation was to be achieved through the natural leaders of society.[34]

In the Puritan view, even civil magistrates had a role to play in the sanctification process, for God "ruleth by his ministers, and that is the prince first, and under him the pastor . . . the sword ruled in the

[30]Rupp, *Patterns of Reformation*, 128. See also Edmund Morgan, *The Puritan Family* (New York: Harper & Row, 1966).

[31]Perkins, *Works*, 3:670. Cf. Henry Ainsworth, *The Communion of the Saints* (London, 1615) 393; George and George, *Protestant Mind*, 257ff.

[32]William Gouge, *Of Domesticall Duties* (London, 1626) sig. A3.

[33]Ian Breward, *The Work of William Perkins*, 437.

[34]Cf. Peter Lake, *Moderate Puritans*, esp. chaps. 3 and 12.

hand of the one, and the word preached in the mouth of the other."[35] Perkins declared that the principal duty of the magistrate was "to urge men to the keeping of the commandments of the first table, to a practice of pure religion and to the keeping of the sabbath day. This is the main duty of the magistrate, who bears the sword specially for the good of men's souls."[36] There is no indication that Perkins or his contemporaries perceived any tension between this emphasis on magisterial coercion and the Puritan emphasis on religious experience, an emphasis clearly present in Sabbatarianism's call for the private Sabbath exercises of preparation and meditation.

The function of all the natural leaders of the social hierarchy in the process of Sabbath sanctification is best summed up by Peter Barker:

> Thou that art a father or mother, and hast under thee son or daughter; thou that art a master or mistress, and hast under thee man-servant or maid-servant; thou that art a magistrate, and hast under thee proselytes and people of another nation: thou and thou, and thou must have a care to hallow the Sabbath, and here that is in this rank, they which are superiors, have the first charge, my note is this: that they must begin to their inferiors, be like the he goats before the flock, excel in virtue, as they do in place, be like the master bee, the fairest in all the hive; first be leavened themselves, then leaven their charge. The precious ointment on their heads must run down by the beard to the skirts of their garments; happy children, happy servants, happy strangers, that can trace their parents, their masters, their governors by such a favour."[37]

Leaders in authority must set good examples, for "the other parts are distempered, if the head be sick." But their responsibilities do not end in themselves. They "must see, that they which are under them follow it, their care must begin at themselves, but not end there."[38]

For the Puritan, the Sabbath was a microcosm of Christian life. Sabbath rest offered an opportunity for intense sanctifying activity, which was typically divided into four phases: preparation for worship; public

---

[35]Thomas White, *A Godly Sermon Preached at Paules Crosse on Sundaye, the 9th Daye of December, 1577* (1578) 36.

[36]Breward, *Work of Perkins,* 463. Cf. John Penry, *Three Treatises,* ed. D. Williams (Cardiff: University of Wales Press, 1960) 60, 61.

[37]Barker, *Learned and Familiar Exposition,* 235, 236.

[38]Ibid., 236.

worship; reflection, study, and conference; and deeds of mercy. Theologically, the familiar Pauline pattern of sin, deliverance, and gratitude is discernible in Puritan Sabbath observance. As "ground is prepared for the seed," a personal spiritual inventory must be taken before going to public worship, an inventory that focuses on "how the week has been spent, what sins have been committed, what graces received, what blessings especially needed."[39] Greenham urges examination of "how we have gone forward in godly proceeding, or how we have gone backward."[40] The doctrine of "preparation for grace," a distinctive mark of Puritan thought in the following century, is reflected in this Sabbath exercise. It is especially apparent in this statement from Greenham: "For what is the cause why in the prayers of the church we so little profit? What causeth the word to be of so small power with us? Whereof cometh it that the sacraments are of such slender account with us? Is it not because we draw near to the Lord with uncatechized hearts, and uncircumcised ears, without prepared affections, and unschooled senses?"[41]

With the heart prepared, Sabbath sanctification continues in the public sphere of communal worship. Here the preaching of the Word is regarded as "the greatest part of God's service," for it is the primary means of salvation.[42] "For there the Lord doth offer unto His church those most notable and singular means of their salvation, which as they cannot want, so they can find nowhere but there, for there is the preaching of the word, which is God's own arm and power to save all them that believe, in so much that without the ministry and preaching of those, that have the public authorities and callings of the church, most ordinarily men are not saved."[43] The sacraments are also to be used to confirm the Word. However, emphasis on the sacraments in Sabbatarian literature is conspicuously less than the emphasis on the proclaimed Word.

---

[39]Bound, *Doctrine of the Sabbath*, 195.

[40]Greenham, *Works*, 359, 360.

[41]Ibid., 360. Regarding the doctrine of preparation for grace, see Norman Pettit, *The Heart Prepared* (New Haven: Yale University Press, 1966).

[42]Bound, *Doctrine of the Sabbath*, 174.

[43]Ibid., 176.

Hearing *and doing* is the Sabbatarian theme. The good words issue into good works. As Greenham puts it, "The Lord his Sabbath is not a day of knowledge alone, but of love; not only of hearing the word by preaching, but also of doing the word by practising."[44] Andrewes, in fact, refers to the life of service as "the great end of the commandment, that His name may be sanctified in us." God "is so delighted in no work, as in the work of mercy," says Andrewes, and there is a "special affinity betwixt sanctification and works of mercy."[45] Greenham remarks that works of mercy are the Christian's obligation every day of the week, "yet especially they belong to the Sabbath, wherein we make a supply of the wants, which we have on the week days."[46] So we are to visit the sick, comfort the imprisoned, feed the hungry, clothe the naked, and bestow our goods on the needy. Bound also lays heavy stress on this dimension of the Sabbath when he states that "all things comprehended in the other commandments must be practised upon the Sabbath," and "all is ceremonial without these fruits appearing in us afterwards." Although we may "come to the church all our life every Sabbath, and remain there from the beginning to the ending, yet only so many days, and no more have we kept holy as we ought, by how many have been bettered and furthered . . . and made more fit to serve God and our brethren."[47]

Creation, Resurrection, and sanctification are the central themes in Sabbatarian literature. Sabbatarian theology was Trinitarian theology, for the three themes find correspondence in the three persons of the Holy Trinity: Father, Son, and Holy Spirit. Appropriately, these themes are heavily accented in the Reformed, Calvinist tradition, especially the doctrines of Creation and sanctification. Puritan theology did not diminish redemption or justification by grace. It did subtly shift the emphasis to the creational context of grace and to the sanctifying means of grace. This shift is discernible in the doctrine of the Sabbath. In the

---

[44]Greenham, *Works,* 366.

[45]Andrewes, *Moral Law Expounded,* 350.

[46]Greenham, *Works,* 366.

[47]Bound, *Doctrine of the Sabbath,* 186-88.

Puritan worldview, God the Father established the Sabbath when he created the world; by his Resurrection God the Son reestablished the Sabbath as the Lord's Day; and God the Holy Spirit uses the Sabbath as the chief means of sanctification.

8

SABBATARIANISM
AND THE
PURITAN VISION

ENGLISH SABBATARIANISM WAS NOT, as anti-Sabbatarians charged, a clever Puritan-presbyterian scheme designed to undermine good order and established authority in the Church of England. The movement was rather the outgrowth of high Sabbath views that had been around for a long time in England and that flowered into full-blown Sabbatarianism by the end of the sixteenth century. In the effort to disentangle Puritanism from the origins of Sabbatarianism, however, one should not be blinded to the important theological, ecclesiastical, and practical connections between the two. The Sabbatarianism that flowered at the end of the century was largely a Puritan creation. It even had some relationship to Presbyterianism. This concluding chapter will show that Sabbatarianism fit perfectly into the moderate Puritan vision for a more genuine and complete reformation of the English church and commonwealth. First it will be helpful to review briefly the familiar story of some major sixteenth-century developments in the Elizabethan church.[1]

---

[1]See Patrick Collinson, *The Elizabethan Puritan Movement* (Berkeley and Los Angeles: University of California Press, 1967); Charles George and Katherine George, *The Protestant Mind of the English Reformation* (Princeton: Princeton University Press, 1961); Patrick McGrath, *Papists and Puritans* (London: Blandford Press, 1967).

From the time of the Elizabethan settlement when, as William Haller says, the queen simply swept many abuses under the rug instead of performing a major church cleaning,[2] there were influential leaders in the Church of England who were dissatisfied with the limited extent of its reformation. Many of these malcontents had spent time on the Continent experiencing first hand the more radical reformations of such centers as Geneva and Zurich. This experience played a large role in the origins of English Puritanism; for when these exiles returned to England upon Elizabeth's succession, they longed for a church purified of all Roman Catholic vestiges, one modeled after the early New Testament church and the "best Reformed churches on the continent." Even earlier, under Edward VI, disputes had arisen over such liturgical matters as the use of vestments by the clergy. That battle was rekindled in the 1560s under Elizabeth. The liturgical controversy continued to smolder for years—in fact, on into the next century—but in the 1570s it was obscured by a related issue that took center stage: the controversy about church government. The vestments debate had raised questions about ecclesiastical authority and where it should properly reside, leading naturally into the presbyterian controversies of the 1570s.

The 1580s saw the development of the "classis movement," defined by Collinson as "an association of puritan clergy of the Elizabethan Church in an organization of ministerial conferences in some sort resembling, and for a period actually styled as, the *classes* and synods of the presbyterian church polity which its members hoped to establish in the Church of England."[3] Collinson shows that the classis movement was related to the earlier "prophesyings" of the 1560s, the small conferences, made up chiefly of Puritan clergy, devoted to biblical interpretation and preaching. They were a response to what was probably the single greatest challenge facing the Elizabethan church: the development of a competent preaching ministry for the thousands of new Protestant parishes. This challenge was, in varying degrees, the concern of the entire leadership of the church and not simply that of

---

[2]William Haller, *The Rise of Puritanism* (New York: Columbia University Press, 1938) 8.

[3]Patrick Collinson, "The Puritan Classical Movement" (Ph.D. diss., University of London, 1957) v.

the Puritans. But in terms of relative intensity, the concern for a preaching ministry became increasingly identified as a Puritan concern by the end of the century, and stood at the epicenter of the Puritan vision.

This classis movement began, not so much by calculated scheme and grand national design as by a kind of spontaneous combustion of area conferences of Puritan pastors somewhat on the order of the prophesyings. These conferences gradually became more formally organized and the member pastors began to style their activities explicitly as "classes" in an underground presbyterian movement. They even became loosely federated into a nationwide organization of classes. John Field was a key figure in this attempt to bring national unity and order to the scheme.[4]

Ironically, Whitgift's promotion to archbishop in 1583 stimulated the movement. Collinson says, "It took Whitgift's general assault on non-conformity to stir this embryonic organism fully into life."[5] There appears to have been widespread support for the Puritan vision throughout the country, and Whitgift's hostility drove sympathizers into the presbyterian movement even if they were not enthusiastic about it. His campaign for uniformity intensified in 1588 after the publication of the devastating, satirical attack on the clerical establishment in the Martin Marprelate tracts. Richard Bancroft, who later would become Whitgift's successor, became the chief investigator of Puritan-presbyterian activity in this period. In 1590 the classis movement was effectively suppressed when Thomas Cartwright and eight other leaders were arrested and brought before the High Commission for extensive interrogation. A year later they went to the Star Chamber for trial. Although they were eventually released without being either acquitted or convicted, it appeared that the presbyterian dream was shattered.

It was precisely in these decades of the 1580s and 1590s that Sabbatarian momentum increased, evidenced by more sermons on Sabbath abuse, more concern about the interpretation of the fourth commandment, and the publication of longer treatises on the Sabbath.

---

[4]Patrick Collinson, "John Field and Elizabethan Puritanism," in *Elizabethan Government and Society*, ed. Bindoff, Hurstfield, and Williams (London: Athlone Press, 1961).

[5]Ibid., 149.

Materially, Presbyterianism and Sabbatarianism seem to be so utterly different from one another that it is easy to overlook the similarities between the two. The precise relationship between aborted Presbyterianism and rising Sabbatarianism is quite subtle. It is not accurate to say, as the anti-Sabbatarians did, that the one was designed to replace the other. There was a latent Sabbatarianism in the Church of England for a long time, and there is evidence of intense concern about Sabbath keeping during the years of the classical movement itself. Nor is the relationship adequately described simply in terms of personnel. While it is probably true that most presbyterians were also Sabbatarians, it is significant that the principal early authors of Sabbatarian treatises were not intimately involved in the presbyterian movement. Lancelot Andrewes was probably opposed to it; even Richard Greenham issued some warnings against it; and there is no evidence that Nicholas Bound was deeply involved in the presbyterian-classical movement.

Presbyterianism and Sabbatarianism were, nevertheless, two species of the same genus: the Puritan vision for further reformation of the Church of England. They operated, however, on quite different levels. Their ultimate goal—a greater degree of reform—was the same, but their proximate aims were quite different. Presbyterianism focused on external administrative forms, Sabbatarianism on the internal spiritual condition. When the more visible political aims of Presbyterianism were suppressed, the reforming activities of the Puritans were limited to the local parish level where the Sabbath was especially relevant. This is not to say that Sabbatarianism had no political implications or manifestations, or that Presbyterianism had no parish relevance. The emphasis of the one, however, was on the administrative structure of the church, and that of the other on the spiritual condition of the people.

What has been distinguished as internal and external dimensions of Puritan reform efforts must not be sharply separated. Because of the various directions of those efforts—liturgical reform, governmental reform, parish-pastoral reform—it is easy to overlook the essential consistency and coherence in the Puritan program. Its leaders did not embark on novel, sectarian tangents for the sake of unnecessarily irritating the church. Puritan concerns were fundamentally interrelated, centering in the spiritual reformation of individuals, families, parishes, the church, and the commonwealth. The ultimate reformation Puritans sought in England was the reformation of people through the proclamation of the Word. In disputes about vestments, church government, and the Sabbath, this goal was all too easily forgotten. The more radical, separatist Puritans lost sight of the ultimate aim, turned means into ends, and succumbed to sectarianism. But for the larger numbers of moderate Puritans, the external means were not at the top of their hierarchy of concerns. They could accept gracefully, though with some reluctance, conformity in ceremonies and episcopacy in church government because they regarded external forms as quite incidental to the more important end of England's reformation.

The bottom line of Presbyterianism, as with Sabbatarianism, was its emphasis on the minister's relationship to his congregation, and on the faithful preaching of the Word to effect real change in the depth of people's lives. A change in church government was deemed desirable to achieve this goal. Their ultimate aim was not itself so controversial, but ironically the means to the end got all the attention, creating division and adversary relationships. So it was precisely the collapse of the presbyterian movement that allowed the fundamental spiritual concerns to flower in more visible form.

It is widely accepted that when the early presbyterian effort failed, the Puritan movement in the 1590s was so weakened that it almost disappeared. This is hardly the case; it continued to function quite powerfully, but on a less visible historical level—the level of the parish. This has led others to say that the Puritan movement went underground.[6] But that image is misleading. Puritanism in the 1590s did not go underground; it simply stayed at home, working diligently for the reformation of individuals, families, parishes, and villages—engaged not in warfare with prelates, but in the warfare of the spirit with the world, the flesh, and the devil. This was not a new direction for Puritanism. This kind of local, reforming effort had gone on all along, and spiritual struggle was the essential warfare from the beginning. Historians' preoccupation with the more dramatic and easily documented events such as the presbyterian movement has diverted attention from the steady, dedicated work at the parish level. Ironically, in the final analysis the greatest potential for reformation lay at that level. And it was at this local parish level of pastoral Puritan piety that Sabbatarianism came to play such an important role.

---

[6]Ibid., 181.

The Protestant Reformation brought about a profound shift of emphasis away from symbol and imagery as vehicles for communicating the faith to *words* as the primary means. In no wing of the Reformation is this more evident than in English Puritanism. At the heart of the Puritan vision was the Word of God and its faithful proclamation by the godly preacher. The "real energy" of the Puritan movement "was supplied by the preacher," says William Haller,[7] and Irvonwy Morgan argues that "the essential thing in understanding the puritans is that they were preachers before they were anything else."[8] Paul Seaver is right when he says that "it is not in the admonition to Parliament or in the academic debates but in the sermons preached from hundreds of puritan pulpits that the puritan ideology was set forth in its totality."[9] The kernel of moderate Puritanism was the godly learned preacher who sought the reformation of faith and morals, and encouraged the inner spirituality of his parishioners. The presbyterian movement might be suppressed, but the Puritan preacher in his parish pulpit still reigned supreme. As long as there was access to the pulpit, there was hope for reformation.

There was a long tradition of complaint about an adequate ministry in the Church of England dating back to William Tyndale. In the 1530s he urged all English clergy to become competent preachers. Accomplishing this noble aim, however, was another matter. Under Henry VIII, Parliament adopted the Act of Supremacy in 1534, thereby "protestantizing" the church. But a half century later, in 1583, only one out of six English clerics was licensed to preach. There were 9,244 parishes at the close of Elizabeth's reign in 1603, but only 4,830 of the clergy were licensed to preach.[10] "Duties neglected, nepotism, plurality, non-res-

---

[7]Haller, *Rise of Puritanism*, 15. Cf. Michael Walzer, *The Revolution of the Saints* (London: Weidenfeld and Nicholson, 1966) 115.

[8]Irvonwy Morgan, *The Godly Preachers of the Elizabethan Church* (London: Epworth, 1965) 11.

[9]Paul Seaver, *The Puritan Lectureships* (Stanford: Stanford University Press, 1970) 5.

[10]Roland G. Usher, *The Reconstruction of the English Church* (London: D. Appleton and Co., 1910) 1:241. See also Ian Breward, *The Work of William Perkins* (Appleford: Sutton Courtenay, 1970) 35ff.; Albert Peel, ed., *The Seconde Parte of a Register* (Cambridge: Cambridge University Press, 1915) 2:89ff.

idence, self-indulgence, some immorality, and, above all, ignorance—these were characteristic of the Church and clergy of the period."[11]

Undoubtedly one of the greatest problems and challenges of the English church was to develop a preaching ministry. This problem was far more pressing in England than in the more localized reformations on the Continent simply because the English Reformation was national in scope. It was a problem intensified by the political aspect of the Reformation in England. Henry VIII's decision to make thousands of village churches "protestant" almost overnight could not await the long, slow process of developing a protestant preaching ministry. Samuel Gardiner, commenting on the situation a few decades later, says, "In most parishes, the very men who had sung mass in the days of Mary now remained to read the service from the Book of Common Prayer."[12] Even the system to produce a trained ministry took a long time to develop. There were no formal theological programs of study in the universities, only informal catechizing by "godly fellows." At Cambridge, however, the moderate Puritan, Laurence Chaderton, worked hard to make preacher training a more integral part of the university curriculum.[13]

Puritans were not the only ones who sought to meet the challenge of providing a more competent preaching ministry. All English Protestants agreed that a Reformed minister's task was to proclaim the Word, pouring it into the hearts and souls of his congregation. John Jewel said that the day "whereby the way and entry to the kingdom of God is opened unto us, is the word of the Gospel and the expounding of the law and the Scriptures."[14] And the preface to the first Book of Homilies stated, "How necessary it is that the word of God, which is the only food of the soul, and the most excellent light that we must walk by in this our most dangerous pilgrimage, should at all convenient times

---

[11]Paul A. Welsby, *Lancelot Andrewes*, (London: SPCK, 1958) 65.

[12]Fuller, *History of England*, 1:28.

[13]Patrick Collinson, *A Mirror of Elizabethan Puritanism* (London: Dr. Williams Trust, 1964) 7.

[14]John Jewel, *An Apology of the Church of England*, ed. J. E. Booty (Cornell: Cornell University Press, 1963) 28.

172   H O L Y T I M E

be preached unto the people."[15] Archbishop Grindal also gave high priority to preaching.[16]

Relatively speaking, however, the intensity of the preaching emphasis is especially associated with the Puritan strain in the Elizabethan church. Indeed, the concern is evident even earlier in godly preachers such as John Hooper and John Bradford in the days of Edward VI, a factor that explains the rise of the prophesyings in the early years of Elizabeth's reign. Moreover, as we have already suggested, Presbyterianism itself is the church-governmental corollary to a high conception of the ministry of the Word, for the sovereignty of the Word preached from the parish pulpit will not brook interference from magistrate or prelate.[17] The principle of the parity of the clergy lies implicit in *sola scriptura*. By the end of the century, the Puritans had developed a reputation for especially heavy criticism of the church's nonpreaching clergy, while conservatives such as Whitgift and Hooker were defending "reading and sacrament" ministers.

For the Puritans, the original sacrament was the preaching of the Word. They believed profoundly in the real presence of Christ in the Bible, and considered the Lord's Supper a dead ritual without this original sacrament.[18] Philip Stubbes wrote, "As the soul is the life of the body, and the eye is the light of the same, so the word of God preached is the life, and light, as well to the body, as the soul of man."[19] William Whitaker in effect reduced all marks of the true church to one: pure preaching.[20] And John More, who preached "almost every day in

[15]*Two Books of Homilies*, ed. J. Griffeths (Oxford: Oxford University Press, 1859) 3, 4.

[16]John Strype, *The Life and Acts of Edmund Grindal* (Oxford: Clarendon, 1821) 561, 62. Cf. Patrick Collinson, *Archbishop Grindal*, (London: Jonathan Cape, 1979) 197ff., 240-41.

[17]Cf. Collinson, *Mirror of Elizabethan Puritanism*, 25.

[18]John S. Coolidge, *The Pauline Renaissance in England*, (London: Clarendon, 1970) 142. Cf. Calvin, *Institutes*, 4:1:5; 4:3:1. See also David Little, *Religion, Order, and Law*, (Oxford: Blackwell, 1970) 68-70.

[19]Philip Stubbes, *Second Part of Anatomie of Abuses*, ed. F. J. Furniwall (London: N. Trübner and Co., 1877-1879) 76.

[20]William Whitaker, *Praelectiones* (Cambridge, 1599) 387ff.

the week . . . and every Lord's day three or four times,"[21] argued that God gives faith by "the preaching of the word, for so he saith, *Faith cometh by hearing, and hearing by the word of God;* and least we should think it were a sufficient means the hearing of the word read, he addeth and saith, *Who can believe without the hearing of the word preached?"* So "the Lord hath appointed to save his people by preaching," and since that is the divine scheme of things, "Alas, what shall we say to the state of the people here in this land? Scarcely the twentieth parish hath a preacher, and can they be saved then?" Let the "blind guides, I say, be removed, and true preachers placed in their rooms," proclaimed More, and he threatened God's judgment on the authorities if they should fail in this task. He concludes, "Unless there be preaching, the people perish: unless they have believed, they are damned, and believe can they not without preaching."[22]

It is not mere coincidence that some of the earliest formulators of Sabbatarian doctrine were among the chief critics of the English clergy. The concern about preaching and the rise of Sabbatarianism are indissolubly linked. Lancelot Andrewes is an excellent example. In his catechetical lecture on the fourth commandment, he includes a lengthy, passionate plea for raising up a learned ministry. He believed it was vital to the health of the nation. Mighty empires had fallen as a result of moral decay, but in other cases, he says, "that which did keep the people from perishing, is *Prophetia,* the careful looking to prophecy." Andrewes observes that in Britain there was also much corruption: "And we see by experience, that our enemies would invade us at such places, where the people are least taught the fear of God." It is impossible to ensure by law "that a man should not be covetous, that there should be no idleness, no riot, pride, etc. . . . Sobriety must first be begotten in the mind: else politic justice will not be." That is why "all manner of sin is soon brought in there, where there is no prophesying." So it is that there must be places of training for a godly ministry. A good precedent existed, for the "first college" was established in the Old Testament, as 1 Samuel 19:18 indicates.[23]

---

[21]John More, *Three Godly Sermons* (Cambridge, 1594) epistle dedicatory.

[22]Ibid., 66-69. See also William Gouge, *The Whole Armour of God* (London, 1627) 155ff., 245ff., 269ff.

[23]Lancelot Andrewes, *The Moral Law Expounded,* (London, 1642) 301ff.

Some years later, in 1593, Andrewes delivered the convocation sermon at Canterbury. He railed at the clergy, describing them as "sitting
still, half asleep, lukewarm, and tongue-tied."[24] Preaching was in a
sorry state, he claimed, and it was not improved by forcing incompe-
tents to preach. "Since the dumb-dogs were lately beaten, every dunce
took upon him to usurp the pulpit, where talking by the hour glass,
and throwing forth headlong their incoherence, . . . they have the luck
forsooth to have it called by the name of preaching. . . . The very
Church is infested with as many fooleries of discourse as are commonly in the places where they shear sheep."[25]

Perkins was another severe critic of a nonpreaching ministry, calling such clerics "dumb dogs that cannot bark," an insult apparently
derived from Isaiah 56:10.[26] His plea was for the "plain" sermon, and
he supported that plea by writing "The Art of Preaching," the first extensive Puritan treatise on this subject.

Bound also criticized the nonpreaching ministry. This arch-Sabbatarian authored the preface to the sermons of John More, which emphasize so forcefully the need for preachers. Interpreting the fourth
commandment, Bound declares that preaching the Word is "the greatest part of God's service" and hence is "unseparably joined to the Sabbath." Since this is the case, it is nonpreaching ministers who chiefly
cause dishonoring or transgression of the Sabbath. It is in the public
assembling of the church that God offers his people "those most notable and singular means of their salvation . . . for there is the preaching of the word, which is God's own arm and power to save all them
that believe, in so much that without the ministry and preaching of
those, that have the public authority and callings of the Church, most
ordinarily men are not saved."[27] People cannot understand the redemptive message of the Scriptures "except we have a guide to preach
unto us."[28]

---

[24]Welsby, *Lancelot Andrewes*, 64.

[25]John Strype, *The Life and Acts of John Whitgift* (Oxford: Clarendon, 1822)
3:293ff.

[26]Perkins, *Works*, 1:55; 3:24.

[27]Bound, *Doctrine of the Sabbath*, 170.

[28]Ibid., 178, 179. Cf. *Sabbathum Veteris*, 322ff.

The anti-Sabbatarians saw clearly this link between the Sabbatari-ans and the emphasis on preaching. "Sabbaths and sermons" were welded together, in the opinion of George Abbot,[29] and John Pock-lington complained later that if you give the Sabbatarians their Sab-bath, you have to give them also "the service that belongs to their sabbath." This was a service that tended to neglect the Prayer Book in favor of preaching. "What service then must you allow them for their sabbath? Why nothing but preaching." He suspects, in fact, that the "Common Prayer book" is "clean cast out of their Sabbath, and no ser-vice allowed or used but preaching."[30]

The preaching of the Word, then, was viewed both as "God's own arm and power to save," and also, as in Andrewes's view, the means to greater godliness in the land.[31] Justification and sanctification both depended on it. Preaching was the primary means of grace—the grace not only of forgiveness but also the grace of godliness. The godly preacher aimed at reformation not primarily on broad institutional lev-els, but on the parish level of personal piety. He would have his people walk with God.

> By walking with God, I mean, a sincere endeavour, punctually and pre-cisely to manage, conduct, and dispose all our affairs, thoughts, words and deeds; all our behaviours, courses, carriage, and whole conversa-tion, in reverence and fear, with humility and singleness of heart, as in the sight of an invisible God, under the perpetual presence of his all-seeing, glorious, pure eye; and by a comfortable consequent, to enjoy by the assistance and exercise of faith, an unutterable sweet commu-nion, and humble familiarity with his holy majesty: In a word, to live in heaven upon earth.[32]

Through a faithful, "painful" preaching and pastoral ministry, this Puritan goal would be reached. Richard Greenham, the prototypical Puritan parish pastor, saw it this way: "And surely if men were careful

---

[29]George Abbot, *Vindiciae Sabbathi* (London, 1641) sig. A3.

[30]Pocklington, *Sunday No Sabbath*, 8.

[31]Irvonwy Morgan, *The Godly Preachers of the Elizabethan Church* (London: Epworth, 1965) 102.

[32]Robert Bolton, *Some Generall Directions for a Comfortable Walking with God* (London, 1626) 29, 30.

to reform themselves first, and then their own families, they should see God's manifold blessings in our land upon Church and Commonwealth. For of particular persons come families; of families, towns; of towns provinces; of provinces whole realms: so that conveying God's holy truth in this sort from one to another, in time, and that shortly, it would so spread into all parts of this kingdom."[33]

Against this background of emphasis on the preached Word, we can appreciate and understand the monumental importance given the Sabbath. The Sabbath itself held sacramental significance, for if the preached Word was regarded as the primary sacrament, or the primary means of grace, the Sabbath was regarded as the primary means of that means of grace. Greenham, in his catechetical exposition of the fourth commandment, alludes to the intimate connection between the Sabbath and the means of faith no less than six times.[34] Public worship was the heart and soul of the day for the Sabbatarians, with the Word being central. All else, including the private exercises, revolved around the Word. It is no accident that most of the authors of Sabbatarian treatises were parish pastors or, as in the case of Andrewes and Perkins, skilled preachers and practical theologians with a keen appreciation for the importance of the proclaimed Word in the parish. Indeed, most of the Sabbath treatises themselves were originally sermons.

The Puritan vision for further reform through the preaching of the Word encouraged the development of strict Sabbatarianism. It was a means to bring people into the churches where the Word was proclaimed. Every Sabbatarian treatise appealed to the recognized and accepted agents of social control—from the monarch down to the householder—to carry out their special responsibilities regarding the Sabbath by urging all within their jurisdiction to go to church. In this way, a quiet revolution could be instituted without upsetting the social structure and without the need for political change. Throughout her reign, Queen Elizabeth consistently rejected the more radical parliamentary proposals for further reform. Sabbatarianism could bypass that step because although there were also parliamentary proposals for

---

[33]Greenham, *Works* (1599), 164.

[34]Greenham, *Works* (1612), 75.

better Sabbath observance, Sabbatarianism operated primarily at the grassroots level—that is, within the existing political structures and with the use of the well-established and accepted leaders in English society, especially the local householders. On the practical side, Sabbatarianism was designed to achieve further reformation by bringing all the people under the tutelage of the Word of God.

As we observed in the previous chapter, Sabbatarianism also brought about the spirituality that became so important in the Puritan vision. For sixteenth-century moderate Puritanism, that vision was not political but spiritual, with a powerful emphasis on personal piety and devotion.[35] One Puritan author after another declared that personal sanctification depended on the Sabbath. "The very life of piety is preserved by a due sanctification of the Lord's day. They put a knife to the throat of religion, that hinder the same," wrote William Gouge.[36]

The earliest articulators of Sabbatarian doctrine saw the fourth commandment in this light. Perkins listed the profanation of the Sabbath among the leading sins of the nation. He added, "[It is] so great a sin that where it reigns, in that country, congregation, family, man or woman, there is no fear of God nor any true grace in them. For keeping of the sabbath is the maintaining, increasing and publishing of religion."[37] In his lectures on Revelation Perkins wrote, "Therefore we must learn to sanctify the Sabbath of the Lord, for else we shall never increase in faith, knowledge, or obedience as we should; for the begetting and increase whereof this day hath been set apart and sanctified from the beginning."[38]

Sir Simonds D'Ewes no doubt spoke for thousands of English Protestants when he wrote in his autobiography that the Sabbath "was the main groundwork upon which I build the practice of all other pious

---

[35]Charles Hambrick-Stowe, The Practice of Piety (Chapel Hill: University of North Carolina Press, 1982).

[36]William Gouge, The Whole Armour of God, (London, 1627) sig. A2.

[37]Breward, Perkins, 294.

[38]Perkins, A Godly and Learned Exposition . . . upon . . . Revelation (London, 1606) 45.

duties."[39] John Ley called it "the training day of military discipline," containing "the sum and substance of all religion."[40]

A more familiar and appealing metaphor was *marcatura animae*, the market day of the soul. The soul was nourished by products from the market of the Word: "Again, it is the market day of our souls, wherein we come to God's house the market place, to buy the wine and milk of the word, without money, or money worth. How is that? By hearing and harkening to God's word, that truth whereby we are sanctified, John 17:17, and to pray unto him; thus by the word and prayer we are sanctified."[41]

George Walker saw the Sabbath as "the hedge of defense to true Christian religion." He wrote that through "preaching, reading and hearing of the word . . . true piety, and the true knowledge and worship of God, and true faith in Christ, are upheld, maintained, increased and continued among all Christian nations from generation to generation." Without the weekly Sabbath, he added, the "most effectual ordinary means of grace and furtherances to eternal life and blessedness, would undoubtedly grow out of use, and at length utterly decay and vanish."[42] He could hardly have made a clearer statement of the Sabbath as means of the means of grace.

In this context, the fourth commandment became the most important of all the moral laws controlling Christian life. The Sabbath was the primary means for the promotion of all righteousness and obedience in the lives of the people and hence the primary means to complete reformation throughout the church and the commonwealth. Cawdry and Palmer declared, "We may call the Sabbath and the due observation of it, the compendium, or continent of all religion: Hereupon it is very observable, that as the commandment of it, stands in the heart of the decalogue as the bond of both the tables, so it is in other places of scripture joined with the chiefest duties of both."[43]

---

[39]Quoted in Mark H. Curtis, *Oxford and Cambridge in Transition* (Oxford: Clarendon, 1959) 187.

[40]John Ley, *Sunday a Sabbath* (London, 1641) sig. C4.

[41]Henry Burton, *The Law and the Gospell Reconciled* (London, 1631) 64.

[42]George Walker, *The Doctrine of the Sabbath* (Amsterdam, 1638) sig. A2.

[43]Daniel Cawdry and Herbert Palmer, *The Christian Sabbath Vindicated* (London, 1645), Epistle to the Reader.

The Sabbath came to be regarded as the cornerstone not only of the kingdom of God but also of the kingdom of this world in the Deuteronomic vision of the Puritans. Henry Burton saw it this way: "So as from the right sanctification of the Lord's day doth spring all holiness, and power of religion, whereby God is honoured, the commonwealth itself is made glorious as being established and combined with the most firm bonds of pure religion, the crown and security of kings and kingdoms."[44] Cawdry and Palmer attributed not only England's spiritual blessings but also its temporal ones to the maintenance of a strict Sabbath. Even material prosperity "began to be clear, when the doctrine of the Sabbath was owned as the doctrine of the Church" in the "Homily of the Place and Time of Prayer."[45] Moreover, the Sabbath was used not only to serve the cause of further reform, but also to explain the failure of the past reformation in England in spite of so many years with the gospel. Another comment from Cawdry and Palmer is typical of this sentiment: "We think one main cause of these national Judgments, under which this land now groans, was the public toleration of the profanation of the day." They are referring to King James's *Book of Sports.*

All time was holy for the Puritan, who believed that all time belongs to God. In a certain sense, every day was a holy day for the Puritan; for as God used the six days for divine work, so he provided six days for the ordinary work of divine calling. But the Puritans were realists who recognized, with a keenness unsurpassed in Christian history, that religious discipline takes special time. Therefore, alongside the time for vocational duty, there must be an especially sacred time for those acts of worship and devotion that are indispensable to any religion. If some sacred time is not set aside, these essential duties will never be done.

And were it not, that the Lord's day did succeed in place of the Sabbath, the Sabbath day of the Jews being abolished; what time for the means of our sanctification and salvation were left unto us? Were it not for the Lord's day, we should be in a far worse case, than the Jews of old, as being left without opportunity and means of sanctification, all which the Lord's day ministreth unto us; without this, we should have no market

---

[44]Burton, *Law and Gospell Reconciled,* 67.

[45]Cawdry and Palmer, *Christian Sabbath Vindicated,* sig. A2.

day for our spiritual provision and merchandise of our souls, where to
buy the pearl of the kingdom, and to supply all our spiritual wants."[46]

Such convictions about the need for a special, holy time were not
merely products of human reasoning. God knows what is best for his
Creation and those who inhabit it, and God himself designed a sacred
time. The Bible tells us so in the fourth commandment, which, together with the nine other commandments, constitutes the bedrock of
the moral universe. For a people to ignore or abuse this holy time is to
lash out foolishly against that universe and against the Creator. God
gave the Sabbath and designated it as an especially holy time wherein
his people could condition themselves for better performance of their
most fundamental obligations, which are spelled out in the other commandments and summed up in the admonition to love God above all
and their neighbors as themselves. No wonder that the keeping of the
Sabbath law was regarded by the Puritans as the key to all the others.
No wonder that, in their Deuteronomic vision, the welfare of the entire nation would stand or fall with the use or abuse of this holy time,
with success or failure in performing the sacred duties of preparing for
the Word, hearing the Word, reflecting upon the Word, and "doing"
the Word. And no wonder that the appointment of such a critical time
could not be left to the relatively untrustworthy discretion of sinful human institutions. John Sprint's ode to the Sabbath sums it up beautifully:

A doctrine harmless, true, and holy, making thee holy and preparing
thee to heaven, agreeing to the Scripture, to right reason, to common
civility, and even to civil policies. A doctrine conforming us to the commandment of God, yea even to his blessed and holy image. A doctrine
bringing much glory unto God, and benefit to man, knowledge to the
ignorant, sense unto the hardened, direction to the willing, discipline
to the irregular, conscience to the obstinate, comfort to the conscienced,
and bringing none inconvenience in the world. A doctrine that addeth
face, fashion, growth and firmitude unto a church, strength and comely
order to a commonwealth; giving propagation unto the gospel, help and
vigor to the laws; ease, honor, and obedience unto the governors; unity
and quiet to the people; and lastly, certain happiness and blessing to
them all. For the which doctrine whosoever argues, pleadeth for GOD,
for his glory, for his worship, for his commandment and will, for his

[46]Burton, *Law and Gospell Reconciled*, 65.

word, his sacraments, and invocation: for the law, for the gospel, for Moses, and the prophets, for Christ and his apostles, for the upholding and flourishing estate of the church and commonwealth, of schools and universities, and of the faithful ministry of Christ. In a word they plead for the wearied bodies rest, for the evil conscience quiet; for the sound practice of godliness and mercy, in a certain, settled, and constant order. And so by consequence for heaven itself.[47]

The Jews had called it "Queen Sabbath" centuries before. By the seventeenth century the Sabbath—even for moderate Puritans—had become queen in England. And if ever the day should come when their allegiance to another monarch might clash with their obligations to this one, there would be no question whom they would first serve.

---

[47]John Sprint, *Propositions, Tending to Proove the Necessarie Use of the Christian Sabbaoth, or Lords Day* (London: Thomas Man, 1607) 35, 36.

INDEX